# Stresshacking

## 50 SIMPLE STRATEGIES TO GET YOUR LIFE, YOUR MIND AND YOUR MOJO BACK

## LOUISE LLOYD

First published in Great Britain by Practical Inspiration Publishing, 2020

ISBN   9781788601672 (print)
       9781788601665 (epub)
       9781788601658 (mobi)

Practical Inspiration
PUBLISHING

MIX
Paper from
responsible sources
FSC   FSC® C013604
www.fsc.org

To my amazing parents and friends:
I love and appreciate you dearly.
To you, the reader: I sincerely hope this book
helps in some way.
And to *love*; to us all living as it and for it.

# TABLE OF CONTENTS

*Acknowledgements* ........................................................ *ix*
*About the author* .......................................................... *xi*
*Introduction* .............................................................. *xiii*

**Part 1: Essential hacks to get you going** ..................... **1**
#Hack 1 – As best you can ...................................... 3
#Hack 2 – Take ownership ...................................... 5
#Hack 3 – One moment at a time ............................ 7
#Hack 4 – And breathe… ...................................... 11
#Hack 5 – Freedom to choose .............................. 16
#Hack 6 – Information detox ................................ 20
#Hack 7 – Pimp your ride ................................... 23

**Part 2: Taking back control** ................................... **27**
#Hack 8 – The good, the bad and the ugly ............ 29
#Hack 9 – Easy, tiger! Managing your freeze,
                   fight and flight reactions ..................... 32
#Hack 10 – Body alert! ......................................... 35
#Hack 11 – Addressing the cause .......................... 38
#Hack 12 – Taking charge of your diary ................ 42
#Hack 13 – People stuff ....................................... 46
#Hack 14 – It's good to talk ................................. 51
#Hack 15 – Navigating awkward conversations ...... 55

**Part 3: Hacking your work stress** ........................... **59**
#Hack 16 – Work–life balance? ............................. 61

#Hack 17 – Working with heart and soul...............65
#Hack 18 – Finding your golden hours..................68
#Hack 19 – Targets and goals .............................71
#Hack 20 – Bin the bitching................................74

**Part 4: Living more mindfully** .............................. **77**
#Hack 21 – Being aware in the moment ...............79
#Hack 22 – Live and let live ..............................85
#Hack 23 – It is what it is .................................88
#Hack 24 – All change......................................91
#Hack 25 – What's done is done.........................95
#Hack 26 – Loosening the grip on the future.........99
#Hack 27 – Thank you!....................................103

**Part 5: Being you** .................................................. **107**
#Hack 28 – Be you!..........................................109
#Hack 29 – Don't fall for your overthinking ........112
#Hack 30 – Facing fear .....................................115
#Hack 31 – Life outside of your comfort zone .....119
#Hack 32 – Calling out your own-worst-
            enemy-self.......................................126
#Hack 33 – Becoming your own-best-friend-self... 130
#Hack 34 – R.E.S.P.E.C.T.................................134
#Hack 35 – Perfectly perfect .............................136

**Part 6: Self-care**...................................................... **139**
#Hack 36 – Give yourself a break........................141
#Hack 37 – Born to move..................................145
#Hack 38 – Posture power .................................147
#Hack 39 – Body love........................................151
#Hack 40 – Fuel your brilliance ..........................154
#Hack 41 – Zzzzzzzzzzz's....................................158

#Hack 42 – Money, money, money ..................... 161
#Hack 43 – System overhaul .............................. 164

**Part 7: The inside job** ........................................... **167**
#Hack 44 – Self-mastery ..................................... 169
#Hack 45 – Hack into inner peace ...................... 175
#Hack 46 – You're so much more than
                    you think ........................................ 181
#Hack 47 – Beyond duality ................................. 185
#Hack 48 – We're in this together ....................... 192
#Hack 49 – The world is your mirror .................. 195
#Hack 50 – Shifting your internal state .............. 197

*Afterword* ................................................................ *201*

# ACKNOWLEDGEMENTS

A huge thank you to Alison Jones and the entire team at Practical Inspiration Publishing along with Newgen Publishing UK, without whom this book would not have been possible.

I knew what I wanted to share but I had no idea how to bring it all together into a book and they have all held my hand and made it happen. Thank you!

I am lucky to have amazing parents and friends and it is their love and support that has stood by me throughout my whole life; writing this book was no exception.

Without meaning to sound vague, and I don't say this lightly, I must acknowledge the many people whose paths have met mine throughout life. I have learnt, and continue to learn, so much from every encounter, however long or brief. This includes the many clients and people from all walks of life that I have had the pleasure to work with over the years. You all inspire me to do the best that I can and be the best I can be.

I would like to acknowledge anyone that I have in any way hurt or impacted negatively. I am sorry, and you too inspire me to become better. I continue to learn.

And finally, I acknowledge *love* itself; it is behind all that I do, all that I am and all that I wish to become.

# ABOUT THE AUTHOR

Louise Lloyd is a mindset and wellbeing coach. Through speaking engagements, coaching and *The Inspired Zone Podcast*, she helps people to hack stress, limits and lifestyles. Louise is on a mission to stop stress and fear getting in the way of people realizing their potential and leading healthy, happy lives.

From CEOs and business owners to coders, scientists and PAs, her practical and effective approach helps people to overcome the challenges they face. She leads sessions for global senior leadership programmes, helping leaders to maintain presence and focus amid pressure.

Having ridden for Great Britain during her career as a professional event rider, Louise knows what it takes to handle pressure and to navigate life's inevitable ups and downs. Her interests in all things mindset began in the 1990s when she was introduced to meditation. The practice gave her significant insight into transcending an overthinking mind and fear, something she has been helping others with ever since.

Louise's background in teaching yoga, meditation and breath practices informs her understanding of the simple and transformational tools that she shares today. She has become the go-to person for many people in moments of crisis or when they feel stuck in life.

Through her interest in helping people move past the boundaries of their comfort zones, she has helped thousands of people to overcome fear, anxiety and limiting mindsets, enabling them to take back control of their lives and go for their dreams.

You can find Louise at www.louiselloyd.life

# INTRODUCTION

*Stress is your wake-up call.*

Let me say this from the outset: things can change. I know you don't know me yet, but please trust me when I say that they can.

Whether you're a busy working professional feeling overwhelmed with work pressure, a parent trying to meet the demands of a crazily busy life, or you are fed up with how you think and feel, then know that it can all change. Whatever the reason behind you coming to the point of reading this book, I am glad that you did.

I want to show you that it is possible to be busy without being stressed. To be successful without burning out. That you can be challenged without being overwhelmed.

You have gifts and talents to share and I want to help you to remove everything that gets in the way of you doing that. I want you to be the amazing person that you truly are and to find all the love, peace and fulfilment that you deserve.

At times, we all find ourselves out of our depth in life. We all have the potential to become stressed, ungenerous and fearful. Too often, we are our own worst enemy and lose sight of who we know we can be. I don't want that to happen. I care deeply about us hacking through anything that gets in the way of us being the amazing human beings that we are. I want that for all of us, and for the world that we live in. Beyond all of the stress that you may currently feel, it is your true nature to be kind, generous and loving. You have a unique brilliance to bring to the world that we live in – even if you don't recognize it.

So however far off that feels for you right now, I know that's who you are. Through this book we will unpick it all together, openly and honestly.

Let the stress that you feel be a brilliant opportunity to reboot your life and to live the life you are here to lead. Stress is not our enemy; it's a sign that something needs attention. Our error is ignoring it. Doing so leaves us needing pills for chronic conditions and aches and pains, and it gives us sleepless nights. Ignoring it ruins our relationships, our confidence and our quality of life. I hope that as you read this book you will see that you don't have to put up with a life led by stress.

Stress is your call to action.

I will guide you through dealing with the causes and symptoms of stress so that you can get your life back. You will become more at ease at being yourself. Of course, there are times in life when things happen that do cause overwhelming stress. I hope that the tools in this book will help you to navigate your way through such times; they have certainly helped me to navigate my way through mine.

I've called this book *Stresshacking* for two reasons. The first reason is that I know that it is possible to hack through the causes of stress – to kick them into touch in a powerful and effective way. I have used all of the tips and tools in this book, both personally and with the many people I have so far helped, so I know the potential they have to change people's lives. The second reason is a nod to my previous horse days, when a hack meant going for a nice ride in the countryside and, rather like many of the hacks in this book, I love that it implies the ease and steadiness of a hack in that way.

The focus of this book will be you.

I will help you to reorganize your inner world and your outer one. Of course, the book will cover practical day-to-day *how to's*, but it will also prompt some soul-searching for you to find the peace and joy that you seek. We can't always control what life brings, and sometimes we most definitely wouldn't choose what it does bring. But we can choose what we bring to life. Every single thought, word, choice or action has an effect. In owning them, we become masters of our own destiny.

In Part 1 you will find some essential hacks to immediately breathe a bit of space into whatever challenges you are facing and into however you are feeling. These hacks alone will help you to find more ease. Part 2 is about taking back control over your life. It will help you to unpick how stress affects you and give you the tools to start addressing what needs to change. In Part 3 you will hack into workplace stress and find the tools to help you to deal with the pressure of heavy workloads and looming targets. Part 4 gives you the tools to start living more mindfully and to free yourself from overly ruminating on the past and the future. Parts 5 and 6 are all about you – they will help you to know yourself, to trust yourself, and most importantly to love and care for yourself. You'll learn to ditch your own-worst-enemy-self and become your own-best-friend-self. Finally, in Part 7, through guiding you into your inner journey, you will learn how you create the outer world that you live in. If you do this inner work you will never be the same again – and neither will your life.

You will notice a theme throughout. *Everything is very simple.* It's all doable – even though you are busy, even though you are tired, and even though you are stressed. You probably feel like your life needs a miracle to change it. That miracle is easier than you think. It can happen through the small, seemingly insignificant, everyday choices that you make. With one small step after another, you can shift your life into something completely different. Something better. Something more fulfilling.

Throughout this book I share strategies and tools that I have both learnt and applied, and continue to learn and apply. I do not claim to be *the* expert or have *the* answer. I invite you to take what you want and leave what you don't. That said, without action all knowledge is wasted. Nothing will work if you don't try it. You have to give it a chance. You have to give yourself a chance. So if you take one thing away from this book then please do something different to what you are currently doing. If you do that, your life will change.

Once a worrier, not always a worrier.

A leopard can change its spots.

You can be comfortable outside of your comfort zone.

You can become your very own best friend.

You can completely change your life.

*Part 1*

# ESSENTIAL HACKS TO GET YOU GOING

*I know of no more encouraging fact than the unquestionable ability of man to elevate his life by conscious endeavor.*

Henry David Thoreau[1]

I love this quote because I have seen so many people do exactly what it describes. It is undoubtedly encouraging that it is possible for us all. Whatever your life looks like right now, know that it can change. If you're stressed out and can't see the wood for the trees, know that this can change.

These essential hacks are here to breathe a bit of space into your everyday life. They are so quick and simple that no matter how busy or stressed you are, you will be able to do them. In doing so, they will begin to make life more manageable.

From this moment on, every time you feel anxious, stuck, hurt, uncertain, depressed, frustrated or stressed, say to yourself these three essential words:

## *This can change.*

---

[1] H. D. Thoreau, *Walden*, 1854, Chapter 2.

# AS BEST YOU CAN

Before we go any further, I want to start with a bit of encouragement.

> I want you to know that you are doing the best that you can.
> You always have done, whether it feels that way or not.

Whatever life is like for you right now, remind yourself of this every single day. Get up each day and make a promise to yourself simply to do the best that you can. Just that day. Exactly as it is. With whatever you face. Irrelevant of any outcome.

I don't say that lightly or flippantly. Maybe you don't handle the day as well as you'd like to, but you're just going to give it your best shot anyway. Don't waste any of your energy beating yourself up on all that you can't do and all that you think you're doing wrong. Just do what you can, as best you can. End of.

# # The hack

In every moment that you are struggling, lovingly remind yourself that you are doing the best that you can.

# TAKE OWNERSHIP

I don't know what is going on for you or what's causing your stress, but I suspect that you don't feel in control of your life right now.

The reality is that much of life is out of our control. By its very nature, life is made up of all manner of experiences and feelings. There will be joy, pain, happiness, sadness, confusion, clarity, struggle and ease. It will continue to twist and turn and every now and then it might literally side-swipe us.

With life sometimes seemingly doing its own thing, it can be easy to forget that we have a choice in what *we* bring in response to it. That's the bit that is in our control but we forget that. We waste time and energy on things that we can do nothing about. In the name of your own sanity, I urge you to interrupt that habit.

Taking control of your life is about owning it. It is about accepting what is in your control and letting go of what isn't. It's about letting go of what you think you *should* be doing, or *could* be doing, and focusing on what you *are* doing. Take full ownership of what *you* bring to life. Own your state of being, your thoughts, your words, your choices and your actions. Every one of them. Don't blame them on anything or anyone else ever again. Why? Because that's the most self-empowering, life-changing thing you can do for yourself.

As you reflect on this, don't beat yourself up about what isn't working. Don't waste time and energy focused on what anyone else is or isn't doing either. Just focus on *you* and your life, as it is right now. So often we spend time and energy focused on what isn't in our control, on the what-ifs. Don't. Not right now, anyway. The best use of your time and energy right now is to focus fully on *you*. What you do. Or what you don't. From now on, take full responsibility for what you can actually do something about.

## # The hack

Take full responsibility for your state of being, your thoughts, your words, your choices and your actions. Don't judge them, beat yourself up about them or get disheartened by them – simply own them, exactly as they are.

# ONE MOMENT AT A TIME

If you've got a lot going on in life it can feel overwhelming. One of the reasons people find having a lot to do stressful is that mentally they are carrying their entire day and everything they have to do in it into each and every moment. If they are dealing with a particular stressful situation, they carry it with them in every single moment. No wonder that is stressful; or that it is impossible to be focused. But even the busiest of days or most stressful times can only happen one moment at a time.

A practice that I call the single-breath practice is to take one deep, conscious breath as often as you can throughout the day.

Try it now. Just take one, deep conscious inhale, and then exhale.

That's it. It's that simple. Use it to remind yourself that you can only be where you are, doing what you can, and that you can get through your entire day by taking it one moment at a time. You do not have to do it all at once. It can be helpful to use it as a way to create transitions throughout the day. For example, you can take a deep conscious breath as you arrive at work to mentally transition out of your journey. Or take a deep conscious breath as you arrive at a meeting to bring your full awareness to it. If you notice you have lost focus during the meeting, you can use it again. Use it as you leave the meeting to transition your focus and energy into what you are about to do. If an email comes in that makes your blood boil, take a deep breath (or several) to help you to step back for a moment before you respond. When you leave work at the end of a day, take another breath and mentally finish the day to make your transition into your evening.

Honestly, this simple practice can change your life! I highly recommend trying it for a few weeks. I once gave this practice to a one-to-one coaching client I was working with. As a managing director of a large organization, he was struggling with the pressure of long hours, lots of work-related travel and the multiple demands coming at him from all areas of the business. I suggested that he used the single-breath practice to keep bringing himself into the moment he was in, and to put space between a demand coming at him and his response to it. He said it helped him to recognize that his desire to respond and resolve issues quickly meant he often did and said a lot of things that weren't as effective and productive as they could be. Using the single-breath practice transformed the way he managed both his team and his personal life. I have found it to be life-changing. I use it to bring my focus into the present moment. I ask myself: 'What am I bringing to this moment? Is it what I want to bring to it?'

When you begin to be more fully present, time opens up for you. Busy days feel more manageable and less hassled. You don't have to do your whole future right now; just this moment. That's all. I will help you to do this in Part 4 – *Living more mindfully*.

# Hurrying is a state of mind

Have you ever noticed that when you are pushed for time you feel a bit hurried and a bit impatient with anything that holds you up? Have you also noticed that when you are *not* pushed for time you can feel a bit hurried and a bit impatient with anything that holds you up?! Mmmmmm. Feeling hurried can become a mindset.

Many years ago, I had an *aha* moment about being busy and feeling hurried. It occurred when I was competing and I was running on a treadmill in the middle of a hectic day. I had raced to the gym to fit a 30-minute session in and still had a packed day ahead of me. I noticed that I felt hurried while I was running. Then I had the realization that, whether I felt hurried or not, 30 minutes is 30 minutes. Clearly I had scheduled it into the day so logistically I had the time to do it. Whether I *felt* hurried or not, the time impact on the day would be exactly the same. It was a turning point for me because that was the first time I realized that having a lot to do and feeling hurried are not the same thing. It is possible to be extremely busy and not feel hurried or stressed. It is also possible to not be at all busy and to feel hurried and stressed. It's a mindset shift. If your full awareness is in the present moment and continues to be so, then even the busiest day won't feel hurried.

How often do you race into a meeting a little late, having rushed from another meeting? Do you feel hurried when that happens? How present is your focus when your day is spent that way? For many people, this creates a bit of what I call the jet-lag effect, in that it takes them time to fully arrive in a meeting because their mind is catching up from racing from the previous one. Then towards the end of their current meeting, their focus is already leaking out into their next appointment because they feel the time is running out in this one. If that is a typical day, it means they are rarely fully in any of their meetings. That is a huge disadvantage. The whole day can have a feeling of *trying to catch up*. It is no wonder we miss essential information or forget things when our focus isn't fully there in the first place. Taking a deep breath to bring our awareness into the moment opens up so much more efficiency and effectiveness. It feels so much better too.

## # The hack

Use the single-breath practice throughout the day to remind yourself that you can only be where you are, doing what you can, and that you can get through your entire day by taking it one moment at a time. Whatever you are facing in life, you only have to face it one moment at a time. Use it to bring your awareness into the present moment and ask yourself: 'Am I mentally hurrying right now?'

# AND BREATHE...

When you are chronically stressed your nervous system is constantly on high alert. This means that as you go about your daily life, you are likely to be defensive in all that you do. In the days of being chased by a predator, our sympathetic nervous system was triggered in a fight-or-flight response so that we could survive. Assuming that we survived, and once the predator had gone, our sympathetic nervous system would switch off and our parasympathetic nervous system would take over, bringing us back to homeostasis. The problem with the chronic stress that many face today is that our nervous system stays on alert – meaning that we are always on edge in case of any looming predator, bosses or dodgy people. Chronic stress means our rest, digest and repair system is suppressed so we are not functioning as well as we could be. It is only a matter of time before the wheels start to fall off.

The good news is that we do have an amazing, free tool that we can use to switch this response off. It triggers a relaxation response, allowing our body to get on with rest, digest and repair, while effectively reducing stress. It is so simple that people dismiss it before they have even tried it.

I didn't dismiss it though, and it has completely changed my life.

That tool is the breath.

Yes, of course, we are all breathing, but the way we breathe can have a significant effect on how we feel. When I used to teach yoga, I found it quite fascinating to watch the way people breathed. It was such a clear indicator of those that suffered from stress and anxiety. Upper-chest breathing is common in those that are anxious, and I notice it in many people when I work in various organizations. The tell-tale sign is no movement in the abdomen when breathing, along with tension in the shoulders.

In our natural, most efficient way of breathing, the diaphragm moves freely in the breathing process. As it contracts and moves downwards during inhalation, the stomach naturally moves outwards. When we breathe out, the diaphragm moves upwards and the stomach moves back towards the spine. For various reasons, stress being one of them, the diaphragm ceases to move effectively, and we begin to recruit the shoulder muscles in an attempt to lift and expand the ribcage. While we would recruit these secondary muscles if we were running from a predator; we shouldn't be when sitting at rest.

Practising diaphragmatic breathing (aka belly breathing) can deactivate the fight-or-flight response, triggering the rest and digest part of the nervous system. Importantly, for your sanity and ability to function in the world, this also enables a return of rational thinking and signals to our entire system that we are safe.

Try it now.

Loosely rest your hands on your abdomen around your belly button. Take a deep breath in and notice if your stomach is moving outwards into your hands. As you breathe out, notice if it moves away from your hands, towards your spine. If it is, then you are naturally doing diaphragmatic breathing. If it isn't, you are likely in upper-chest breathing. Your stomach might be doing the opposite; going towards your spine when you breathe in and out towards your hands when you breathe out. This is known as reverse breathing and is another restrictive breath pattern.

To practise diaphragmatic breathing, if you are not already doing so: try gently pressing your stomach outwards towards your hands as you breathe in and then let it relax away from your hands as you breathe out. It will take effort to do this so be patient with yourself. I highly recommend focusing on this breath pattern for a few minutes any time you feel stressed and want to relax. I also suggest doing it for ten minutes before you go to bed at night, and again if you wake up during the night. It is also a great practice to do first thing in the morning to set the tone for a grounded, peaceful day ahead. Trust me – while your hectic day doesn't feel like you have time to do this, it will be life-changing if you do. It's ten minutes. It's doable. Surely worth a try?

## Super-stress buster

Another simple but effective breath practice to relieve stress is to take a deep breath in through the nose and then exhale through the mouth. I call this practice the sigh-of-relief!

Try it now.

Inhale through the nose for a count of four; exhale through the mouth for a count of six. As you exhale, in the words of Elsa in *Frozen*, think to yourself 'let it go' – or as my mum thought she sang, 'let it snow'! Whichever works for you.

If this length of breath doesn't work for you, use a count that suits your natural breath length without bringing strain to it. The exhale should be slightly longer than the inhale.

You might have already noticed that when other people are stressed they do a lot of sighing. Without even realizing it, they are using this tool to help manage their feelings! Next time you get overwhelmed by anything, try taking three or four of these breaths; or more if you need to. It's also a very useful tool to use in times of extreme distress, when in pain or when a panic attack is coming on.

*Please don't underestimate the potential that breath practices have for changing your life.*

They are fantastic for managing the pressures of everyday living. I use the breath on countless occasions: in moments when I need to be fully present; when I am triggered in fear or am overwhelmed; when I am in pain; or when I start to get impatient. I have found that using the breath to put space between how I feel and I how respond to life has been life-changing. It has helped me to interrupt my habitual fight-or-flight reactions. In particular, I used these breath techniques to help me get through the devastation I felt when my husband and I split up. Having never suffered from panic attacks before, I started to get them when something reminded me of him. It was thanks to these breath practices that I managed to stop the panic attacks before they got hold. It affirmed to me just how effective they are.

# # The hack

Practise *daily* belly breathing – ideally for at least ten minutes. But if you're anything like me, then start with taking just five to ten breaths, or whatever you know you will stick with on a daily basis. You don't have to want to do it or enjoy it; you just need to do it. It's so effective in managing stress – if you really want to get a handle of your stress, then I honestly recommend doing it.

Use three or four of the sigh-of-relief breaths any time you feel stressed or overwhelmed, as part of your daily survival kit.

# FREEDOM TO CHOOSE

Life is full of choices. Ironically, as much as that brings vast freedom, it can also create stress from not knowing what to choose. There can be the fear of making a wrong choice, a feeling of overwhelm from having so much choice, or you can forget that you have a choice at all. The fear of missing out (FOMO) can rob us of ever feeling satisfied or at peace with the choices we make. It can be quite a revelation to replace FOMO with JOMO, the joy of missing out (an acronym first coined in 2004 by Anil Dash, a blogger and CEO of software company Glitch).[2] You really don't have to choose everything in life – obvious, I know. But we forget that we are the ones with the choice. Knowing this will allow you to filter your choices, enabling you to live more authentically, to do meaningful work, and to feel fulfilled and alive. It is truly liberating to filter out what you don't want and zone in on what you do. Learning to tune into your preferences over and above anyone else's is a freedom that we sometimes forget we have. Just because things are possible or available doesn't mean we *should* have them, do them or be them. It just means that we *could* if we choose to.

---

[2] Anil Dash's website is https://anildash.com

Learning to recognize what is leading our choices helps us kick stress into touch and to unlock the life we want to lead. The more self-aware we become, the more we feel the tangible difference between making choices through a sense of fear and making them from our loving, true self. When we are stressed we often make choices through fear. This can leave us trapped in a negative cycle of events. Every choice has an effect and is creating the reality we live. That's why the breath practices (see #hack 4) are so valuable when we are stressed. They help to interrupt any knee-jerk, fear-based reactions and choices and enable us to make more supportive ones.

We only have so much time, and what we choose to spend that time on is more of our choice than we realize. We only have so much energy too, and how we use that is also our choice. Then there is how we spend our money. All of these choices are creating the life we are living. What we think we spend our time, energy and money on and what we *actually* spend them on are not always in alignment.

What do you *actually* spend your time, energy and money on?

Is that in alignment with what's important to you? With the life you want to live? If it's out of alignment, it isn't because you mean it to be. It's because you haven't taken control of, or owned, your choices. If you, your choices or your life aren't really how you want them to be, then before you get disheartened know that they can change. *Everything* can change.

The reason I know this is because I've done it myself. I have completely changed my life and who I am. I was previously in a career that I thought was my childhood dream, until the day that it wasn't. After much denial and avoidance of facing that fact, I had to admit to myself that it was no longer what I wanted. While I could have stayed in it, I knew that it didn't fit any more. I was becoming more and more unhappy. I also realized that the person I found myself to be was not the one I wanted to be, or even liked. I was often impatient and tunnel-visioned. I could overthink things and become over-reactive and over-emotional. So I set about changing it all. I plunged into self-development and changed my life beyond all recognition. I always had the belief that I could choose my path in life. That gave me the confidence to literally leave one life and start another. I have also always believed that *we* can change, especially when we want to.

The great thing about living in a world with so many possibilities is that it's never too late to change direction or to create a lifestyle we wish to have. It's never too late to change who we are or how we are. From my own experience, I know that it takes effort and a commitment to change and that it's not necessarily a smooth ride. It starts with taking an honest look at ourselves and our lives, and requires us to become more self-aware. We have to take full responsibility for every choice we make and for how we are responding to life. All of this takes courage and not everyone is up for that. As you are reading this book though, I suspect that you are up for it. Whether you want to be less stressed, don't like who you are, or you're living a life that just doesn't quite fit, you can change it all. I know you can. You just have to choose to.

# # The hack

Start recognizing, and owning, that you have a choice. It's your life. Start to pay attention to what's driving your choices, and whether you are actually making choices that are in alignment with who you really are. Learn to say *yes* when you want to, and *no* when you don't!

# INFORMATION DETOX

We can't ignore the pace of life or the volume of information our minds attempt to process every day as potential causes of stress. In the digital world we now live in, we are fast becoming checkaholics and it is getting in the way of our peace, sanity and quality of actual real life. If your smartphone has become the third person in your relationship, the additional child that you focus your energy on, or the extra workload in your day job, then really think about whether it's worth it.

Have you thought about the amount of extra work your brain has to do just to filter through all of that relentless scrolling? Have you thought about the lost time? I ran a lunchtime session in an organization a few years ago and we were talking about exactly this. One of the participants had said how stressed she was with having too much work to do. When we came onto the subject of smartphones interrupting productivity, someone brought up their screen time app, which this particular participant hadn't realized she had on her phone. When she checked it she had already been on social media for three hours that day! Now, I doubt very much she had actually sat at her desk for three solid hours on social media. More likely, from the moment she had woken up until this session started, she had been checking her phone in between everything she was doing, or trying to do. By lunchtime she had put in three hours of scrolling.

The constant scrolling that many have become addicted to can leave a feeling of anxiety or dissatisfaction in life. While it is easy to blame work for feeling overwhelmed, we can't ignore this voluntary overload of mental processing. Keeping up to speed with everything that everyone is doing is wearing us out. We have to question whether this addiction to being connected to everyone in our online world is robbing us of real-life connection. I am not saying it is, but it might be. Becoming addicted to 'just checking' creeps up on us until we are filling every spare moment with checking something. Before the emergence of mobile technology, those extra moments were an opportunity to be momentarily still; to pause, to take a breath, to process things happening in the day. If you want to significantly reduce the stress in your life, try going a few weeks without having your phone attached to your every move. After the initial withdrawal symptoms, you will likely feel space and peace opening up in your life that you hadn't realized were so readily available.

I should also mention emails here too. Detox your emails by unsubscribing to everything that you don't open or read. Keep your communication succinct when emailing, and don't forget you have the option to pick up the phone, which can turn ten emails into a two-minute conversation.

# The hack

Pay attention to how much time you spend scrolling on your smartphone. Pay attention to what you spend your time, energy and focus scrolling through. Is it worth it? Do you need to do it? Does it add quality to your life? There's no right or wrong here: it's your choice.

Detox your emails.

# PIMP YOUR RIDE

Whatever means of transport you use, journeys can be stressful. But they needn't be. It doesn't seem to matter which way we travel; we are all going to meet busyness and delays sometimes, and that will mean we will at times be late. We have a choice in those moments – to get frustrated and anxious, or to remain calm and make the best of our journey.

When I mention the term *road rage*, people often get a glint in their eye and appear quite happy to be part of that club. I mean, idiots need telling, right? But think about this for a moment. Road rage is a classic symptom of chronic stress. It makes no logical sense at all to get irate with a stranger that you have likely never seen before, nor will again. It makes no logical sense to further endanger your life by getting right up behind the person that has just pulled out in front of you. No logical sense at all, other than to the stressed-out ego which feels totally justified in its rage.

So the question is this – do you let your frustrations and rage get the better of you or do you choose to own your state of being and do something about it to restore calm? Which is better for your overall sense of peace in life? You honestly don't need to get involved in anyone else's driving ability, other than to drive safely yourself and keep out of harm's way. We don't need to battle with anyone on our journeys – only our stress does that. In the words of Elsa from *Frozen* again, next time you get tempted by road rage, see if you have the ability to 'let it go'. Honestly, it's transformative, as I have learnt myself.

So here's my advice on making your journey one that doesn't add to your stress:

1. Allow more time than you think you need. People often create their own stress by not doing this.
2. If you can avoid peak traffic times then maybe that's a better use of your time. I always prefer to get somewhere an hour early and work from there rather than sit in traffic. It's not always possible I know, but if it is it's well worth the extra effort.
3. Go out of your way to be generous to others when travelling. Seriously! This will transform your journey, let alone theirs.
4. Music? Podcast? Audio book? Silent thinking time? What is the best way for you to enjoy your journey? I have to say I am not an advocate of listening to anything engaging or of chatting on the phone (hands free) while driving, particularly in heavy traffic, because I believe focus is best spent on driving. That said, road and traffic condition depending, enjoy your ride!
5. If you get stuck in traffic, or your means of transport is delayed, try not to be in resistance of this fact. It is what it is. The best you can do is stay cool, calm and collected so that when you do eventually arrive at your destination, albeit late, you are still cool,

calm and collected. Best to arrive in that state, ready to be effective and fully present, than to arrive as a frazzled mess that is completely mentally scattered. It's obvious I know, but how often do you arrive somewhere late in a totally stressed-out, scattered state? Late and calm is way better than late and stressed.

# The hack

Your journey is your choice. Own your state of being and do everything that you can to make your journey a stress-free one. Breathe. At the very least, your journeys can become non-adversarial, and at best they can be a really enjoyable part of your day. Even if you don't like travel, you don't have to be at war with it.

*Part 2*

# TAKING BACK CONTROL

If you have been doing the essential hacks in Part 1, you have started to create positive momentum. You have been breathing a bit of space into your life. Every time you feel anxious, depressed, stuck, hurt, lost or stressed, continue to say to yourself the three essential words from Part 1: *this can change.*

Part 2 is about taking back control. It's about recognizing how stress affects you personally and identifying your default fight, flight or freeze response, along with what you can do about it. It will help you to look the cause of your stress in the face and give you the tools to start dealing with it. You will start to take charge of your diary, stop getting sucked into other people's stuff and learn to navigate any awkward conversations that might be long overdue. Ultimately, it's about getting your life back.

The theme of Part 2 will be to ask yourself:

*What needs to change?*
*What can I do to change it?*

# THE GOOD, THE BAD AND THE UGLY

Let me just put this out there now – not all stress is bad. In fact, we actually like some of it because, as humans, we enjoy overcoming challenge. Stress is created when there is a gap between the challenge we face and our ability to meet it.

Positive stress is felt when there is a challenge that might take us out of our comfort zone but we have an overall sense that we will handle it. We recognize the gap and feel equipped to close it. We love working towards something and such challenges can be exciting and energizing. They give a sense of purpose in life and a reason to get out of bed. When we handle a challenge well, it gives us a sense of achievement. It builds our confidence to face future challenges; even spurring us on to seek them out.

Negative stress, on the other hand, is a sense of feeling overwhelmed with the challenge we face. It arises when we don't feel equipped to close the gap and meet it. Money worries, unrealistic deadlines, impossible targets or relationship issues are all examples of things that might create negative stress. The effect of negative stress in our lives can be demotivating and exhausting, and it can diminish our confidence to face future challenges. Most importantly, it gets in the way of us being the amazing human beings that we can be.

Stress affects us all differently. It becomes apparent in the day-to-day choices we make; in our lack of patience; the way that we drive; and in the way we take our loved ones for granted. It shows in our aches and pains, our chronic ailments and our appetite. When we are stressed, an underlying tension sits under everything that we do, whether we see it or not.

Most people get stressed sometimes; it's part of life. The problem arises when we aren't equipping ourselves to meet our challenges. Stress can sneak up on us through the accumulative effect of the many small demands of daily life. Singularly, each of these demands would be no problem but when several begin to accumulate, they can tip us over the edge. It can be a blurred line between coping and not coping. As I am sure you can relate to, even when we recognize that we are stressed it can be tempting to ignore it. We are often too busy or too scared to delve into the real cause of stress and take the actions that would be required to address it. Dealing with the ongoing trickle of daily-life stress will help you to avoid reaching burnout or breakdown.

We will all face times where life will be extremely challenging, if not totally overwhelming. That's being human. A bereavement, accident, divorce or moving house are all examples of situations that may overwhelm us. It's what we do when we are stressed that will make the difference. Some people spend their whole lives either failing to recognize their own stress or trying to ignore it, numb it or mask it. Owning stress is the first step in addressing it. Life isn't about being stress-free; it is about dealing with stress when it arises, in whichever form that is.

Remember that *you* are not your stress.

When we are stressed, we are not the people that we want to be. We can become narrow-minded, less generous and less loving. We might become miserable, dissatisfied and impatient. Often we are less creative, less focused and less productive. We know we are more than that. Nobody gets up in the morning intending to have a bad day. None of us set the intention to look for things to irritate or upset us. We don't intend to pass our stress on to others or to ruin their day. It's worth remembering that. Stress isn't something to be ashamed of or embarrassed by. It is something we should own and address. Stress is our call to action – to get whatever help we need to deal with the challenge that we face.

## # The hack

Identify the cause of your stress. Is it acute stress from a specific situation? Is it the accumulation of the many demands of daily life? Or is it a mindset or belief like a lack of confidence? It might help to write it down. At the top of a piece of paper start with 'I get stressed about...' Just allow yourself to keep writing until you feel that you have emptied it all out onto the paper.

# EASY, TIGER! MANAGING YOUR FREEZE, FIGHT AND FLIGHT REACTIONS

Negative stress causes us to become increasingly on edge. Under stress, we can become emotional, irrational and over-reactive. When stress is left unattended, our whole outlook becomes more negative; we begin to fear the worst in every situation and start to perceive everything as a threat. Eventually, everything has the potential to trigger us into an anxious, angry or withdrawn state.

Our nervous system's response to stress is the same now as it would have been in survival days when faced with a life-threatening danger like a predator. We freeze, we fight or we run. Our nervous system doesn't know the difference between a real-life threat and a perceived one. If we are worrying about something that isn't even likely to happen, our nervous system will respond as if it is happening. If we are triggered by the stress of meeting a deadline, it becomes the predator. We will react in a fight, flight or freeze way. Have you ever noticed that when you're nervous about something, like the day of a big presentation or taking an exam, that you are going to the loo every five minutes before it starts? Yep – that's your nervous system emptying you out so you are ready to fight or run from the predator. Notice that your heart rate goes up when you are being given unwanted feedback? Yep – your heart is pumping blood around your body so you are ready-set-go to fight or run in response to it.

The fight response is reasonably apparent. It might show up as anything from mild irritation through to excessive acts of verbal or physical violence. It served us well when we needed to fight a predator trying to kill us but when it arises during road rage – well, it seems a bit excessive. But in that triggered, irrational, road-rage moment it can feel entirely justifiable to be aggressive – even though that's not who we want to be. In a fight response we attack the situation or person we are having the problem with.

The flight response would obviously have been to run away from the predator. When faced with something that worries us, the flight response might look more like going quiet, denial, burying our head in the sand or withdrawing from life. In the flight response, we avoid the situation or person we are having the problem with.

The freeze response has a benefit in some situations; if we stay still for long enough if faced with a predator passing by, it might not see us and that could save our life. But the freeze response isn't useful if we feel frozen to the spot when it would be better for us to take action.

We all have our 'favourite' triggered reaction; sometimes we combine them all depending on the situation. It is useful to identify your default response. I used to have quite an explosive reaction when triggered, which usually involved a deluge of tears after I had erupted. My unconscious default is to initially get verbally defensive before running for the hills and avoiding the person or situation altogether! Because I don't feel comfortable with conflict, another unconscious default is to try to mediate whenever there is a problem between other people, which can mean I get involved in situations that are none of my business. Self-awareness brings many useful insights that can better inform our chosen response to life. I have found it really helpful to recognize my triggered stress reactions. I have also learnt that taking a few deep breaths to put space between how I might feel and how I choose to respond is invaluable, as is understanding why I have been triggered in the first place.

Gaining more control over our reactivity requires both in-the-moment action as well as longer-term action. Using the single-breath practice or the sigh-of-relief breath from #hack 4 will help in the immediate moment, while practising belly breathing daily for ten minutes will help you to be less reactive in general.

## # The hack

What's your triggered reaction in life? How does it vary from one situation to another?

Next time you notice that you are having a fight, flight or freeze reaction, can you take a few deep breaths? Give yourself a moment. Use the sigh-of-relief breath from #hack 4 to deactivate your fight-or-flight reactivity. Use the daily belly breath practice to become altogether less triggered in life.

# BODY ALERT!

How does your stress show up physically?

Our physical body is witness to everything that we experience in life and will often show us what we are mentally trying to ignore. Poor digestion, inflammatory conditions, colds and aches and pains can all be signs of stress. We seem to have accepted these conditions as part of life without questioning why they are there. We all react differently to stress and part of managing it is in recognizing our own personal signs and symptoms. Our bodies do an amazing job of carrying us through life so it's time we started listening to and looking after them.

The body has a way of getting our attention when our mind is ignoring the messages life is trying to give us. I have experienced this a few times myself. The first time I broke my collarbone at a competition was one of those occasions. I knew I had broken it the moment I stood up from the fall. Although I felt no pain whatsoever, I could feel the bone moving. The power of adrenaline is quite incredible as I felt no pain for a day or two; until it finally hit. I was initially frustrated that I couldn't compete for a few weeks, but then something surfaced that I hadn't realized was there. I felt totally relieved that I had a genuine reason to rest. That I could give myself permission to back off. I didn't know

I felt such pressure until that moment, but clearly I did. That fall gave me a wake-up call. It made me reflect on why I needed something as extreme as breaking a bone to give myself permission to rest. If you can relate to that then please don't wait until your body literally forces you to stop. You will achieve far more in life if you look after yourself.

Another occasion that my body was trying to tell me something was when I was teaching yoga. I was a freelance teacher in various organizations, one of which was a yoga centre. It became apparent to me that this particular centre's owners and I did not have the same values. I started to feel uncomfortable teaching there, and though I tried to resolve matters with the owners, it became apparent that things wouldn't change. As I became increasingly frustrated, my body took over the situation. On days that I was due to teach at the centre, I would get up in the morning and have completely lost my voice. Like, no voice at all; not even a squeak. The next day, when due to teach somewhere else, I would get up and my voice would have returned. This pattern continued until I acknowledged it and quit teaching at the centre. Dis-ease in our mind, thoughts or emotions shows in our body and will often miraculously heal the minute we address the cause of disharmony.

Are you aware of times when your body is trying to tell you something? What needs addressing?

## Soothing the symptoms

Aches, pains and illness are a call for love and care. If your back is aching, it is asking for a massage, some yoga, attention to your posture, to notice what burden you feel in life or maybe to seek expert advice. If you keep getting headaches, they are asking you to notice what mental strain you are under, perhaps your neck and shoulders need attention, or you need to drink more water or get your eyes checked. Maybe you need to see the GP. If you keep getting a bloated stomach, it's a call to check what you are eating and to reflect on what it is in life that you are struggling to digest. If you get out of breath going upstairs, the body is asking you to get fitter, to notice what's suffocating you in life, and to breathe some fresh air into your lungs and some energy and zing into your daily life.

Every symptom in the body is a call to love and care. Every. Single. One.

# The hack

Listen to your body. What is it trying to tell you when it is aching, hurting or not feeling well? What does it need? What do you need? Every action you take to look after your body is worth it... however small. Every action you take to address the physical symptoms of stress is worth it... however small.

# ADDRESSING THE CAUSE

I know it sounds obvious to say this, but if you want to reduce your stress then you need to address the cause of it. You'd think it was a given. But we don't always do that. What we often do is feel powerless and do nothing about it at all. We might manage the symptoms of stress but often only when they get in the way of us 'carrying on as normal'.

So let me ask you: what have you done to resolve the cause of your stress?

Some causes of stress don't have an easy fix and require a longer-term approach. If you tend to be a worrier, for example, you might feel it is 'just who you are' and that it won't change. But it can change. You can change. You just haven't found the right approach yet. I have worked with many people to enable them to drop their worry tendencies. Given the right tools and determination, things can improve. You first need to decide that you want to do something about it. Nothing will change if you aren't actively trying to address it.

## Solution minded

Whenever you face a problem, stress or a challenge, ask yourself if your focus is on finding a solution. Ironically, many people get so wrapped up in thinking that the situation shouldn't be as it is that they forget to actually try to do anything about it.

So, having identified the cause of your stress, ask yourself these questions...

1. What needs to change?
2. What's in my control? What isn't?
3. What outcome do I want?
4. What do I need to help me?
5. Who do I need to speak to about this?
6. What next step do I need to take?

## Symptom or cause?

Sometimes, on the surface, a symptom can appear to be the cause of a problem when it isn't. Drinking too much alcohol or overeating, for example, may cause problems and create a negative cycle of events, but they are symptoms rather than the root cause. The question is: what drives that behaviour? That is the cause. That's what needs addressing. If you just try to use willpower to stop overeating without addressing the reason you are doing it, you will likely stay trapped in the cycle of it. If you feel a lack of self-worth, you will keep creating situations in your life that confirm that to you, until you address your lack of self-worth.

Lasting solutions require hacking the root cause, rather like pulling up the roots of a weed rather than just trimming the leaves. Both the symptoms and the cause of them need addressing. I know that's obvious but it still needs saying.

Are you addressing your symptoms or the cause of them?

# Responding to the cause of stress

I know that sometimes the cause of stress might be a situation that is out of your control. While that can be difficult, let it be a clear message to you to turn your focus to the bit you can control – your response to the situation that is out of your control. If you can't change the situation you face, you have to change the way you face it. Equip yourself to meet it, as best you can. This entire book is about helping you to do that.

Eckhart Tolle, author of *The Power of Now*, says that we always have a choice as to how we respond to any given situation that is causing us a problem.[3] Firstly, is there anything we ourselves can actively do to change it? If there isn't then, secondly, can we accept the situation as it is? We don't have to like it or agree with it but we can accept that it is as it is and that it can't change. Thirdly, if we can't change it and we can't accept it, could we remove ourselves from the situation entirely? Failing to actively choose one of these responses keeps us in a loop of frustration and moves us no nearer to a solution. Not all options are possible for every situation but acknowledging that we are choosing one of them enables us to take control of our response to life.

So, under the wise advice of Eckhart Tolle, ask yourself which of these three choices you are making in your response to the cause of your stress. Can you change it? Do you need to accept it? Or could you remove yourself from it?

---

[3] E. Tolle, *The power of now*, 1999, p. 68.

# # The hack

Ask yourself the following:

*What is the cause of your stress and what are the symptoms of it? Are you addressing both?*

*What can you do about it?*

*What do you need?*

*What is the next step to take now?*

Now take that next step. One step at a time you can deal with whatever you are facing… You've got this!

# TAKING CHARGE OF YOUR DIARY

Before I get into hacking your busy schedule, I want to first say that sometimes life is just crazily busy and there isn't much we can do about it. Whether it's crazy busy because of taking care of kids and parents or an intensely busy period at work, there are times when every last ounce of time and energy is being squeezed out of us. When our to-do list is out of our control, how we address it is the bit that is in our control. It is especially important during these times that we take the day one moment at a time. It is especially important to use the single-breath practice (see #hack 3) to create a moment to breathe.

Do your best to be in flow with being busy rather than wasting any of your energy fighting the fact that you are. Acknowledge that you're crazy busy, but do so lovingly with yourself. Acknowledge that you might be stressed about being busy, but do so lovingly. Don't fight it all. Don't resist it. You can look after yourself in the process. You can, for the time being, accept that this is your current reality, if there really is nothing you can do about it. You can breathe just a little bit more, even amid the chaos. Every time you get overwhelmed at how much you have to do, take a deep breath. One step at a time, you will get things done. One day at a time, you will move through it all. All things pass.

Now, all that said, crazy busy going totally out of control is another matter altogether.

You have to start owning what you choose to spend your time and energy on. Somewhere along the way you need to look at whether all of what you are doing is absolutely necessary, or if it just seems that way.

First of all, let's split the hairs between a must do, should do and could do. A *must do* is non-negotiable use of your time and energy, like I must feed the kids or I must do the work I have agreed to do if I want to keep this job. A *should do* is where we feel obliged to do something, like I should go to the family lunch or I should stay late to finish this assignment. A *could do* is a guilt-free choice where we don't feel obliged, like I could go to a friend's reunion or I could go for a walk at lunch. The trouble is that we mistake many should's and could's with a must do, when in reality they are not. If you want to take charge of your diary then you have to get ruthless about what you choose to do and what you choose not to. You have to become clear about what is totally non-negotiable use of your time, and what isn't.

If you are a people-pleaser (see #hack 13), you need to get comfortable with not pleasing everyone. Trust me when I tell you that your sanity and health need to come above the guilt you feel when you think you have annoyed a few people. Seriously, take it from me to give yourself permission to look after yourself in the process of all that you are trying to fit in. It's not selfish – it's sustainable.

Nobody can tell you what you have to be doing with your time and energy. There are no right or wrong choices here; there are just the ones you decide to make. Are your choices reflecting quality use of your time? Is what you are spending your time and energy on in alignment with who you are and how you want to live? Where are you wasting your time and energy?

Look at your schedule for tomorrow, the coming week and the next month or so – what is a must? Should do? Could do? Be ruthlessly honest. Own what you decide to do or not do.

If you are living a crazily busy life, are loving it and totally thriving – then you go for it! Enjoy it and ride that wave of energy.

If you are crazily busy, stressed out and on the way to burnout – then do not wait for the wave to take you down. You need a radical overhaul of your diary. Refer to #hack 11 to help you to unpick what exactly needs to change and what your next step is in addressing it. Remember, if you are stressed about having too much to do in not enough time then there is a gap between what you are trying to do and what is currently possible. How can you close that gap? What help do you need? What can you cut out of your to-do list? Remember, you can only do what you can humanly do. No more than that.

Another quick tip is on when you say *yes, no* or *maybe* in response to a request. Often when we are put on the spot and asked a 'can you?' or a 'would you like to?' question, we feel pressured into saying yes when we mean no, or we delay a no with a maybe response. I encourage you to get into the habit of using the single-breath practice before you reply. Give yourself enough time to say no when you mean no. To say no when you say maybe but mean no. And of course to say yes when you mean yes! As simple as this sounds, it's life-changing. You won't believe the freedom you feel from learning to be succinct and honest in your response to requests. Try it and see what happens.

# # The hack

Take full ownership of how you spend your time and energy. Get ruthlessly honest about what's a *must do*, *should do* or a *could do*. Use the single-breath practice before you answer with a *yes*, *no* or a *maybe* response to a request. Give yourself permission to look after yourself amid your busyness — it's not selfish; it's sustainable.

# PEOPLE STUFF

One of the significant stresses we tie ourselves in knots around is trying to keep everyone happy. It's a good thing to be considerate of others, to care for and support each other. It's not so good if you are spending so much of your time and energy doing things for others that you are fast on the way to burning yourself out. Or that you are unfulfilled in your own life because you are filling in the gaps in everyone else's.

If you want to reduce your stress and your to-do list, you will need to start supporting yourself a bit more, and that means making a few decisions that work for *you* and your life. I am not suggesting that we turn into selfish narcissists. Somewhere between the extremes of martyrdom and narcissism is the balance of looking out for others and living a fulfilling life.

While a desire to people-please can come from a genuine care for others, often what sits behind most people-pleasing tendencies is a need for approval, a need to be liked and a need to be seen as a *good person*. Sometimes it comes from a need to avoid conflict or a feeling of being at fault and needing to make up for that fact. While it can seem that a people-pleaser's sole intent is to fulfil other people's needs, it is actually a need to fulfil *their own need*. By *keeping* people happy, the people-pleaser themselves feels more at peace/loved/liked/approved of. If you are a people-pleaser, ask yourself what it is you fear if you don't keep people happy. What are you trying to avoid feeling?

I worked with a client who was fast on the way to burnout and was struggling to meet work deadlines. She was near to exhaustion and kept blaming herself for not having the energy to get everything done. Having been asked to work with her to address her workplace stress, it became apparent that she had problems with saying no to anyone or anything, both in work and out of work. When we unpicked things further, it stemmed back to her childhood where her strict father would often come home in a bad mood and consequently row with her mother and be cold and unloving towards her. In an attempt to keep the peace, she used to do jobs to cheer her mother up and would do her best to keep quiet so as not to annoy her father. She worked really hard throughout her education to try to please her father that way, which is where she felt she got some attention from him. Seemingly, to her, if she did everything *right* there was more peace in the house, so that's what she tried to do. That pattern continued into her friendships, where she would do anything to keep the peace, and into her relationships, where she always put her partner's needs above her own. If anyone else was struggling around her, in or out of work, she would try to pick up some of their load.

Fast forward to when I met her, with a full-on high-pressured career, a husband, two teenage kids and two elderly parents, and her people-pleasing pattern had reached a crisis point. It took some work around her beliefs and self-worth before the pattern shifted and she could allow herself to have some healthier boundaries. It took a while before she was able to say no and remain guilt-free about doing so. What she did start to notice, once her new boundaries were in place, is that the time she did spend with people was of a far better quality. She realized that she had stopped enjoying life and had become so used to doing what everyone else wanted that she had absolutely no idea what she wanted. She had got to the point where she didn't even care what she had to eat if she went out for a meal. With her new-found boundaries and energy, she finally started to get a sparkle back again, meet her work deadlines and feel like a human being again.

We can't be all things to all people. Neither should we try to be. Next time you are cramming your diary full of things you *should* do, or think you *have to do*, stop and ask yourself if that's really the case. Family gatherings, reunions, events, socials, this, that and the other – yep, if you want to get back in control of your life, you are going to have to filter them all. Honestly, believe it or not, the world won't collapse if you don't attend everything you are asked to (see #hack 12). It isn't solely your responsibility to keep the whole world's plates spinning. If someone else isn't happy, while you might want to support them, it isn't your job to try to fix life for them.

Next time you find yourself saying yes to things that you haven't got the time or energy for, ask yourself why you are doing that. I'm not saying that there aren't occasions when we agree to do something we would rather not, like going along to something to support our partner, family or friends – but filter the decision. If you decide to go because *you want to support them* then that is different to feeling like you should, or have to, which you do not. You could say no. Helping and supporting others is part of being the caring, loving human that you are – burning yourself out will mean you won't be capable of helping anyone.

Learn to say no. At first, it will feel toe-curlingly, stomach-turningly uncomfortable but with practice you will get better at it!

I should probably touch on taking on other people's emotions and problems. It's often one of the side-effects of people-pleasing, and why we get so drained. It is human nature, thankfully, not to like to see other people suffer (OK, so I know some of you are going to say that isn't 100% true, but let's go with the majority of good people that most of us are). If someone is having a hard time in life, it is natural to want to support them, and it's good that we do, if we can. But it serves no useful purpose at all to take on their mental or emotional stuff yourself. If I was in bed with flu, I might need someone to bring me medicine but I wouldn't expect them to, or want them to, have my flu for me. If someone has just found out they are being made redundant and is going through a whole range of fears and emotions, it is helpful to them if you can be there to support them. It isn't helpful to them or you for you to personally take on how they feel. I know that is obvious but we do need reminding of that.

You can care for someone and their journey in life but you can't do it for them, however hard you try.

There are also some people in life that will suck the life force out of you but don't actually want help. If there is someone at work or in your personal life that is really negative and always wrapped up in their latest drama, you don't have to get drawn into it all. You can help them by listening and by asking them what they want to do about it.

If it becomes apparent that the person really does just like a life of drama, you have a choice not to engage with it. There are better uses of your time and energy. Not everyone wants help, or to change in any way; even though they think they do. We all have choices.

If you find yourself taking on other people's emotions, use the single-breath practice (from #hack 3) to step back from the situation, and to recognize what's their energy and what's your own. You can be empathetic without needing to feel their emotion yourself. Use the breath, and getting whatever space you need, to manage your own mental and emotional state of being so that you are better equipped to support others with theirs. Be aware that when we get triggered by other people's emotions, it is often because they touch upon our own emotional unhealed wounds, and it is those too that are calling out for love.

## # The hack

Give yourself permission to look after your own wellbeing. If you have people-pleasing tendencies, look into what's behind that need. Not everyone needs to like or approve of you.

Learn to say no – by practising it.

Use a few deep, conscious breaths to separate the emotions you are picking up from others from your own emotional and mental state of being. Know that you can't do anyone else's journey for them.

# IT'S GOOD TO TALK

Honestly – it really is. It is true that a problem shared is a problem halved. Sometimes that means talking to friends, family or work colleagues. Other times, it means talking to an expert. It does us good to get things off our chest. Talking things through with someone can often help us to find our way forward, or at least offer respite along the way.

The problem with internalizing stress is that we can end up ruminating over a warped sense of reality. We can find ourselves running internal storylines through the eyes of our fears, and mostly they just aren't true. Before we know it, we have convinced ourselves of a worst-case scenario. Talking to someone will help give us another perspective, options and a way forward. We will realize that we are not alone, stupid or stuck.

That said, it's essential to talk to the right people. It won't help to speak to people that just want to bitch about the issue. It won't help to talk behind someone's back if they are really the person you should be talking to. It does us all good to let off a bit of steam, and sometimes that does mean having a good old moan about someone to our friends or partner. I am just saying that it won't help if you end up on a bitching and moaning loop without actually doing anything to address the cause of your stress. That behaviour is more an avoidance tactic rather than facing the issue. It might give temporary relief but in the long run it won't bring you closer to solving the problem.

Talking to the right people brings comfort and helps us move towards a solution. If we think about stress being the gap between where we are and what we face, speaking to the right person can help us to close that gap. An expert will help us with knowledge that we don't have. A friend will offer support and comfort, which in turn can give us the confidence to take whatever next step we need to. Talking to the person we have an issue with, rather than about them, will close the gap between any misunderstandings. Most importantly of all, talking to people will remind us that we are never alone and there is always someone that can help.

*Be honest.*

If you want to have meaningful conversation with people and you want to be proactive in solving problems then you need to be honest. Completely. You need to be real.

## Do you listen?

A few years ago, I was focusing on trying to be fully present and to listen more during conversations (as part of practising mindfulness, which I cover in greater detail in Part 4). I found that I wasn't really listening to much at all. Superficially, yes, but actually entirely focused on listening, no. It was particularly evident when talking to someone while I was doing something else. It's obvious if we think about it; our focus is momentarily switching between what we are doing and the conversation we are having, so we miss bits of it. I decided that for the duration of this focus I was going to stop doing anything else when speaking to people. I thought that would mean I would then be fully listening but I found that I still wasn't.

I noticed that in many conversations I was trying to listen but was preoccupied with how I would reply. Sometimes I found myself being impatient; interrupting or finishing sentences for people because I thought I knew what they were about to say. Perhaps this subtle level of impatience is a detrimental side-effect of the busy world we live in, where we have become habitually too hurried to listen fully. Albeit unintentionally or unconsciously, we are hurrying people up when they try to speak, and we assume, often wrongly, that we know what they are trying to say.

It isn't just the potential misunderstanding that hurrying a conversation costs us. What is the cost of making somebody feel unimportant or not worth listening to? Taking the time to be fully present in a conversation allows us to hear what is being said. We also notice what isn't being said, which can be even more revealing.

Another thing I discovered was getting in the way of me listening was being too attached to my own agenda. On occasions where I was so focused on the direction I wished the conversation to go, I barely left room for the other person to speak at all, albeit unintentionally. It dawned on me that many of these conversations were, in fact, one-sided: either I was talking, or I was waiting to talk.

The more present I become in conversations, the more that I see all that gets in the way of me genuinely listening. I witness the many layers that can stand in the way of authentic conversation, all of which play their part in us feeling disconnected and misunderstood. Nobody intends to be distracted and disconnected; we just don't realize that we are.

Can you be fully present and hear what another has to say, in a non-judgemental way?

Listening fully, as well as speaking honestly, greatly reduces misunderstandings and the potential stress that arises from such misunderstandings. It is a choice to truly hear another, and it is a choice to switch off from listening to them. Your life will likely be considerably enriched by being fully present during conversations – you may find the side-effect to be one of deep-felt connection and heart-opening humility.

# The hack

It truly is good to talk! Talk to people – don't isolate yourself with your stress and your problems. Think about who the right person to talk to is, and then be honest. You have nothing to be embarrassed or ashamed of. It's also truly good to listen! We are all on this planet together, to help and support each other.

# NAVIGATING AWKWARD CONVERSATIONS

You may find that when you start to address the causes of your stress, you will need to have some potentially, and usually long overdue, awkward conversations. We all have conversations that we find uncomfortable from time to time. Maybe it's an appraisal at work that doesn't go too well, telling your partner that you feel your needs are not being met, or hearing them tell you that theirs aren't, turning down an invitation, or having to make a complaint.

Staying focused and present when having a difficult or awkward conversation is more challenging when we might be triggered by fear. We can find that we're not really listening, or that we get derailed from saying what we mean to. If we are not fully present when triggered into fear, we will likely react in a fight, flight or freeze way. The fight response will dominate the conversation, possibly in a slightly aggressive or pushy tone. During a flight response, we go quiet, often saying nothing at all, or at the very least not what we mean to. If a conversation is particularly upsetting, we might have a freeze response where we feel frozen to the spot, unable to hear or respond at all. The freeze response in these situations may well feel like an out-of-body experience and send us into shock.

First of all, try not to have awkward conversations when there isn't enough time for them. The most successful outcome for any difficult conversation will come about from having it at the right time, in the right place. I know that isn't always possible but if it can be, it will be worth it.

While it is not always possible to prepare in advance for such conversations, it is helpful to do so wherever you can. It can be useful to reflect on what you want to say so that it is clear in your mind in advance of having the actual conversation. That way you are more likely to listen fully and less likely to get swayed from saying what you mean should you get uncomfortable. It isn't just about being clear on what you want to say though; you might need time to reflect on how you really feel before you even think about how to verbalize that.

If you anticipate that you will feel uncomfortable during the conversation, it will help enormously to do what you can to stay calm before you start it. The breathing techniques already discussed (see #hack 4) will help. Once in the conversation, breathing steadily throughout helps to stay present and calm.

Tempting as it may well be, don't hurry the conversation. Take time to hear without interrupting, and give yourself time to respond consciously. Try to stay non-judgemental with the intent to understand and be understood. The single-breath practice is particularly useful to put space between what the other person has just said, how you feel and how you would like to respond. This can prevent blurting something out that you don't really mean.

Allowing steadiness into the conversation helps us to speak truthfully from the heart instead of from a defensive, triggered reactiveness. Being present also helps to differentiate between any emotions that you might be feeling, and the other person's. If you stay present, you will pick up on many subtleties and emotions throughout these conversations. This can be helpful, but not if you get so drawn into them that you lose focus and awareness. You won't feel threatened by differing opinions if you stay present in non-judgemental awareness (covered in more detail in #hack 22). It is only then that a real adult-to-adult conversation can take place.

## Putting yourself in someone else's shoes

I used to think that 'putting yourself in someone else's shoes' was a good thing to do. Through mindful listening, I have discovered that doing so does create limitations. To put ourselves in someone else's shoes means that we think about what we would do in their situation, reflecting on how we would feel if it were us. This is not the same as fully listening to them tell us how it is for them and how they feel. Listening to someone through non-judgement, with the intention to understand them and how they feel, entirely transforms communication. How often do we find ourselves listening to someone from our own perspective? How often do we project our experiences into what they are trying to tell us? Many misunderstandings arise because we assume we know what someone means, or that they understand us. Many problems in life would be solved if we listened to each other in a non-judgemental way with the intent to understand. Remember, it is our true nature to be kind, loving, generous and collaborative – only fear gets in the way of us being that.

# # The hack

Wherever possible, preparation is key to difficult or awkward conversations. Take time to be clear about what you want to say, to be sure that's what you really mean, and then have the conversation at an appropriate time and place.

Recognize that you and/or the other person/people might get triggered into a fight-or-flight defensive response. Try to see past that. Breathe. Do not put yourself in their shoes – listen to them instead. Do the best you can to be the open, loving and patient person that you truly are. Keep the intention of trying to understand each other at the forefront of the conversation.

*Part 3*

# HACKING YOUR WORK STRESS

Work can either bring benefits to our wellbeing, or it can rob us of it. Learning to manage the demands you face and work with a sense of purpose enables you to bring your gifts and talents to whatever you are doing.

If you have become overwhelmed and don't know whether you are coming or going, or you are heading towards burnout, then it's time to hack your work life!

Part 3 will help you to hack into heavy workloads and targets, and to find your most efficient and effective way of working. It can all change.

From now on, when you begin every single workday, say to yourself these three magic words:

## *I've got this!*

# WORK—LIFE BALANCE?

Are you happy with how much time you spend working?

Depending on the work we do, where we do it and with whom, it either contributes to our wellbeing or it can rob us of it. For some people, work is a means to an end – a way to pay their bills, end of. For others, it is a passion and calling that they just so happen to earn a living from. For many, work sits somewhere in between those two points. In any case, most people spend considerable time and energy at work, with the line between work and home life becoming ever more blurred.

For some people, work–life balance is a real problem, while others say that it is all a myth – after all, work is part of our life, not separate from it. When people feel they have a problem with work–life balance, it is because the total number of hours they work feels too much in the context of other things they are trying to fit in. They feel that they spend too much time working and not enough doing anything else. Mobile technology has played a considerable part in blurring the line of 'at work' or 'not at work'. It also has as much to do with the amount of time we are 'at work' in our heads as well as being physically at work.

There is no one-size-fits-all approach to how much time someone spends working. It really depends on what is going on in life and what we want out of work. For a single person that loves their work, living alone, without anybody whose care depends on them, working a 60-hour week might fly by with joyful ease. If that same person were to find themselves in a relationship, it might start to nudge that feeling as they began to want time to do other things. Further down the road, should they find themselves with a family to care for, 60 hours might start to feel like a tight squeeze. Add caring for elderly parents into the mix, and that equation is bursting at the seams. Any sense of balance largely depends on what demands are placed on our time and energy and where we want to spend our time and energy.

The real question is: can we manage the demands on our time and energy, wherever they are coming from? Trying to fit 50 hours of demands on your individual time and energy into 24 hours of real time isn't possible, however good you are at time management. Trying to do it all is stressing people out. Being realistic about what is humanly possible, and putting support systems in place, is a necessary part of avoiding burnout.

Juggling full-time work with looking after the home, childcare, school runs, elderly parent care and other 'keeping life going stuff' is a challenge that shouldn't be ignored. It often comes at the expense of quality rest and play; something that's essential to wellbeing.

What are you repeatedly trying to fit into 24 hours? Is it working for you?

## Heavy workloads and unrealistic targets

Crazy targets and insurmountable workloads can be a major cause of stress. If we relate stress to being a gap between the challenge and our ability to meet it, we can see why these factors are often the cause of stress. It is common for people to feel that they are failing because they are unable to do all of the work that faces them. In the 24/7 world we live in, the sense of accomplishment and satisfaction that comes from finishing a day's work can be difficult to find. When the work continues to pile up, a day's work is seemingly never done. Creating healthy boundaries will make our working lives sustainable, even if there isn't a one-size-fits-all solution. Knowing and accepting that work will keep coming, and that you can only work through it in a humanly possible way, allows you the freedom to work through it all one step at a time. Learning to do what you can, and be at peace with what you can't, leads to greater productivity and less stress. Learning to be honest about what is and isn't possible creates healthy expectations. How often do you find yourself agreeing to do something you know isn't possible? Don't!

A good example of this happened to a friend of mine. They were asked for a piece of work that would take ten hours and were told it was needed in three hours. My friend wisely asked the question: 'Would you like the finished product in ten hours, or would you like what I can do in three hours? Which is it?' While the pressure to promise a ten-hour project in three hours is commonplace, agreeing to deliver it is misleading and creates undue stress.

Is it time we were all more realistic about what is and isn't possible? Until we learn to differentiate between what is a good stretch and what is totally unattainable, we will continue to cause unnecessary stress. A challenge is one thing; denial is another.

I know that targets need to be met to stay afloat. I get that. We all want to stay afloat. I don't think it's right to ignore the undue stress we place on people when unrealistic targets are set. All that said, realistic or unrealistic targets aside, what we can all do is try our best every day, in a sustainable way. All achievements occur by taking one considered step after another; whether a goal or target is set, met or moved on from. Know that the workload will keep coming. It's unlikely to neatly all get done. Do a good day's work. Stop when the day is done. Rest and look after yourself. Then start again tomorrow. Some people happily risk burnout in order to achieve what they want to achieve. There is no judgement here – it's all choice. Just remember *you* have a choice, and that your choice inevitably affects others too.

## # The hack

Review the context of everything you are trying to fit into 24 hours. Does it work? If not, refer to #hack 11 and #hack 12 to address what needs to change.

Pace yourself – heavy workloads get done by working through them one step at a time in a sustainable way.

Stop promising what you know isn't possible. Be realistic about what's a good stretch and what's denial.

Every time you get overwhelmed, breathe and say to yourself these very wise words from Theodore Roosevelt: 'Do what you can, with what you have, and where you are'. You really can't do more than that.

# WORKING WITH HEART AND SOUL

Do you have a job, a career or a way of life?

When I split up with my first husband and needed to earn more money to pay my bills, I worked in several part-time jobs to make ends meet. I waitressed at the local pub, worked as a shop assistant and had a gardening job, all to top up my income. Even though I only did those jobs to pay my bills, I still did them to the best of my ability. In doing so, I took pride in my work and felt job satisfaction. I appreciated the money and the fact that I could sleep at night knowing that those jobs paid my bills. I quit the jobs as soon as I could afford to but that didn't stop me being genuinely grateful for having them and giving them my best. There is something rewarding in giving any job the best that we can. Fair work for fair pay.

Some careers are lifestyle choices, as was the case when I was a professional event rider. I didn't care how hard I worked and I loved it. The hours required were spent by choice, and I would not have wanted it any other way. The 'work–life balance' of any sports professional might appear crazy. An entrepreneur setting up a new business will throw all balance out of the window to achieve what they set out to. Some industries follow seasonal peaks that create similar intensity. None of these offer what some think of as work–life balance but to those who choose that way of life, it is an accepted part of what's required.

We are all seeking a sense of purpose and fulfilment. Often, we seek this externally when in reality it starts internally from what we give of ourselves to that in our external world. It doesn't matter whether you are in a career that's a passionate calling or you are doing a job just to pay your bills. What matters is that you own that choice and that you give it your best. If you can't do that, give your best to finding out where you can. I know that had I not changed careers when I fell out of love with eventing, I would have ended up depressed and ill.

If you are in a job that is stressing you out, do something about it. If you can't resolve it, leave. If you suffer from any form of anxiety, depression or limiting mindset, and that is getting in the way of life, then get help with it. Life is too short to make yourself ill through work-related stress. Without doubt, the workplace can be a significant cause of stress. It is, however, also the employee's job to do the job they have agreed to do. That means remembering that we are there to work and to contribute. The workplace should provide a suitable environment for employees to thrive, and it's our responsibility to ensure we are fit for work. That means that we take responsibility for our own wellbeing, mental health and ability to do the job.

Success in our work life looks different for us all. It is about being authentic to who we are, and our work is part of that. Everything in life has a cause and effect. Work is part of life, in whichever form it takes, and will have its good points and its not-so-good points. It is about weighing them up and making our own choices. We live in a world where it is possible to re-train, re-educate or change careers. We could work more hours, fewer hours, remotely or flexibly. Don't waste your life choosing someone else's career or work life; choose your own. Maybe you don't like your current job but you don't know what else you could do. It is worth exploring what that might be, and in the meantime appreciate your job for keeping a roof over your head. Maybe you won't be there forever but while you are, put your energy into it. Do your best. It's your true nature to do that.

# # The hack

Give your best to whatever you are doing, whether that's a job to make ends meet, a developing career path or a total career lifestyle. Own your choice to be there and accept that there will be aspects of any job or career that aren't your favourite thing to do, but put your best efforts into them anyway.

Remember the *change it, accept it or leave it* response to any situation from #hack 11. Whatever you do, don't stay in a situation that you don't like and moan about it. You know you are better than that and life is too short to voluntarily stay in resistance to that which we choose.

# FINDING YOUR GOLDEN HOURS

There are certain times of the day when we are at our peak alertness and creative genius. Times when our best work flows effortlessly out of us with maximum efficiency. Then there are times of the day when things feel sludgy, heavy and uninspired.

I am a morning person, so if I wake up at an ungodly hour full of inspiration and energy, I get up and use it. Quite regularly I will wake up at 4 or 5am, get myself a cup of tea and my laptop and then get back into bed to work. These are my golden hours where, like an alchemist, I turn raw material into gold. By 9am I have fired through an amazing amount of divinely inspired work with the day still ahead of me. By the evening, that inspired energy has usually left my planet and I rarely attempt to do anything that requires focus or inspiration during that time.

When are your golden hours?

I know this sounds obvious, but using our peak hours to do our most pressing or important tasks is the key to producing our best work in a sustainable way. Any time you get behind with work and need to push hard to catch up, I suggest that you use an hour or two of your peak wakeful state to lock into your work in an undisturbed fashion.

# Flow state

Creating opportunities to get into a flow state is essential if you want to produce gold. There are times when we really do need a *do not disturb* sign to allow us to get into an uninterrupted flow. It's in that state of flow that our creative genius resides. You cannot expect to get into that state if you keep answering calls, emails and messages, or keep scrolling through social media. I know that being interrupted is a normal part of most people's working lives and that is OK for some of the work. It isn't OK when you need to get into a zone. It isn't OK when you need to tap into divine inspiration.

There is no one-size-fits-all approach to where you work best in flow, but you need to identify where and how you can create your own personal flow zone. What time of day is best? Do you need silence or background noise? Do you need to be on your own or surrounded by people? Where is the best environment for you? Remember, the goal is to produce the best-quality work that you can, in the most efficient, effective way that you can. The same applies to team flow zones, which is often why going off-site works so well.

# Multi-tasking

I know we think we multi-task and I know that apparently we don't actually do that; instead, we switch focus quickly from one thing to another. That switch takes time and effort. While it is a normal part of everyday life to switch from one thing to another or to try to do several things at once, I want to throw the idea into the mix that the less we do of that perhaps the better. The problem is that multi-tasking can become a habit. I often wonder whether people really need to multi-task all day or whether it is their lack of focus that invites it in. Like starting six tasks and flitting from one to another, meaning six tasks are all partly done, rather than any finished. Or the habit of watching TV while also scrolling through social media, while also looking at emails, or also Googling random stuff.

So, without labouring the point, it might be worth checking in with your multi-tasking and identifying which is necessary and which is just habit, albeit a less efficient one. Do you need to check emails all day long or is there a more efficient way of getting through them? Do you need to answer the phone every time it rings or is it best to filter calls? Do you need to read and reply to a message immediately? Like everything, there isn't a right or a wrong approach. There is the approach that works for you.

## # The hack

When are your golden hours? Try doing your most important or pressing tasks at that time. Use the same golden hours when you need to catch up on work that you are behind with. Check in with your multi-tasking – when is it needed and when is it an inefficient and avoidable habit?

# TARGETS AND GOALS

In the goal and target-orientated world that we live in, it might seem counter-intuitive to loosen your grip on outcomes and results. Of course we want to meet targets and goals. Of course we want to achieve our best and move beyond previous limits.

The problem is if we get too attached to outcome, we tighten up. We limit our ability. How often has somebody made it to the top of their game but struggled to stay there? The pressure felt when there is so much to lose can easily ruin performance and peace of mind. Mastery comes from being able to let targets and goals sit in our awareness but yet we maintain the ability to be fully in the moment – to be in the state of flow. I know I have produced my best competitive results from that state. Learning to perform under pressure relies on the ability to get present and get on with the job in hand.

Loosening the grip around outcome isn't about lacking desire or care, or losing sight of achieving a goal. *It isn't that at all.* Instead, it is the true ownership of staying in the present and giving our best, moment by moment, whatever the result. In doing so, we become capable of achieving our highest potential. For those of you that need a bit more convincing about loosening your grip on outcome, I recommend reading Michael Singer's book, *The Surrender Experiment*.[4] He is testimony to just how much can be achieved by surrendering all attachment to outcome. Throughout the book, he describes the synchronistic events that happen when we surrender to giving our best to life as it unfolds. In following that approach he has built more than one multi-million-dollar business, which is living evidence that loosening our grip can produce outstanding outcomes.

There is no denying that having targets to meet is pressure. Letting that pressure ruin our performance and our life is optional. You can keep the target in perspective and keep bringing yourself back to what you can do, in the moment you are in, to increase your chances of meeting it. If you waste time and energy worrying about achieving the goal, you will be less productive, less creative and less effective. Breathe. Break it down into doable steps. Get present. You will find a joy and simplicity in working towards targets or achieving goals moment by moment.

The other interesting benefit from loosening your grip on the outcome is the impact *not* reaching a target or goal has on you. There is a quicker turnaround in moving forward positively. You are less devastated. It doesn't mean that you don't care, or that you can't take any learning from it. On the contrary, it means that you can identify what you have learnt and proactively move forward enriched by it. When we have become too tightly attached to a particular outcome, we can be totally bereft if it doesn't come to fruition. It can completely wipe our confidence and leave

---

4 M. Singer, *The surrender experiment*, 2015.

us on the floor, struggling to pick up the pieces. Loosening our grip around an outcome, goal or target will reduce this suffering and help us to move forward. I am not saying that we shouldn't go all in to achieve things in life. What I am saying is that not everything will go to plan and that our life isn't over if it doesn't.

# The hack

How tightly do you grip your goals and targets? If you feel fear around them, then you are limiting your potential. Breathe.

What would it feel like to allow yourself to loosen your grip of them enough to enable you to simply keep giving your best to each moment on the way to achieving a goal or target?

# BIN THE BITCHING

There can't be many people that haven't had a good old bitch about someone. We've likely all been there – you know, when we let off steam about all the things someone else is doing, has done, will do, shouldn't do, has no right to do, we can't believe they do, does intentionally, says and shouldn't say.

A rant. And often we temporarily feel much better for having had one.

The problem is that it doesn't really solve anything.

Perhaps instead of the rant – or as well as – a better use of our frustration would be a greater exploration around what could be done to resolve the situation. Or to reflect on how *you* responded to the situation that pressed your buttons. Should you be having a chat to the person you are bitching about, for example? Or reflect on why they are triggering you so much. What is behind your negativity? After all, despite whatever the person has done that you are bitching about, it is now *you* who is being negative in bitching! What is it that they mirror to you? It is often said that what annoys us in another is an aspect of ourselves that we are in denial about. I have certainly found that to be true in myself.

Remind yourself that, at heart, you are kind, loving, generous and understanding. Your true nature wouldn't need to bitch. So if you have been triggered into bitching then you have abandoned who you are. Breathe. Refer to #hack 11 to address the cause. There will always be things and people in life that periodically press our buttons. There lies the opportunity – owning our response, no matter what. No matter how triggered.

I have had countless conversations with people in organizations who, when on the subject of what causes them stress, will literally let rip at how their manager and/or boss is being totally unrealistic, inconsiderate, unappreciative and, in short, making their life a total misery. When I ask them what their manager had said when they had the discussion with them about all that wasn't working, they will often reply to me that 'there's no point trying to speak to them, nothing will ever change'. Well, I agree; it won't if nobody has a clue that that's how someone feels. Contrary to belief, managers are rarely mind-readers. Nor can they do anything about what they don't know about. Instead of employees bitching about them to other agreeable members of the team, if they *really* wanted to resolve the issue they would be speaking to the manager, not about them.

Similarly, it can happen in friendship groups. How often do friends have a bit of a bitch about something one of the *friends* has done, is doing or is being like? Instead of actually talking openly to the friend, which is what you would think friends are for, the rest of the friendship group just discuss it among themselves. I know there is an element of wishing to avoid awkward conversations (see #hack 15), but when we stand back from the situation it really does seem quite bizarre that this sort of thing happens so frequently. How about lovingly having that awkward conversation with the friend about your concerns, finding out why they are doing what they are doing, making sure they are OK, asking if you can help at all?

Bitching, and all negative gossip for that matter, becomes a habit. Sometimes we don't even know we are doing it. Put it on your radar. Set the intention to catch yourself in the act and, when you do, ask yourself if it serves a purpose. Would it be better to be talking to the person, rather than about them?

On the subject of negative gossip... Have you ever considered that if you enjoy a good gossip, you could have a positive one?! You could gossip about the great things that people do, or how amazing someone looks today, or how you could help the person you know who is having a hard time. I suspect you will get the same feel-good-factor that you get when you engage in negative gossip. You will likely shift your whole day into a much more collaborative, enjoyable one, not to mention that you will also be being the truly amazing person that you already are. Just a word of warning though... you may well find that anyone hell-bent on being a moaner will avoid you like the plague. Mmmmmm, food for thought!

## # The hack

Catch yourself in the moment when you are negatively bitching or gossiping about someone. Could you talk *to* them rather than *about* them? Is what you are saying moving you any nearer to a solution? What's your call to action?

Try positive gossip as an alternative to negative gossip. The world is full of amazing people doing amazing things. That surely is worth talking about.

# LIVING MORE MINDFULLY

Life happens one moment at a time. You don't have to do it all at once. Somewhere in between everything that's happened in the past, and everything that will arrive in the future, is the life you are living now.

Life is happening in every moment. Our quality of life will be determined by our ability to fully participate in it.

Part 4 will help you to do just that. To live your life consciously, now. It will help you to let go of the past, live life in the present and embrace the future when it arrives.

It's all very simple really, as we will unpick throughout Part 4. It's just about you making the choice to be and say:

## *I'm here, now...*

# BEING AWARE IN THE MOMENT

To have any control over our life, we have to first become consciously present in it. Being present in the moment interrupts any habitual unconscious choices and reactions. Through being fully present, we begin to notice how we feel, what we are thinking and what we are bringing to life. We become aware of the same in the people around us and of the impact we have on each other.

Being fully present is the essence of mindfulness; a topic that has become increasingly popular. Given the hyper-connected world that we now live in, this growing popularity is perfect timing. Amid the frenzy of non-stop demands on our attention is a calling from within us to steady the craziness. We crave peace as much as we crave fulfilment.

Mindfulness enables us to settle into being where we are, fully participating in what we are doing and being who we really are. It invites us to fully accept and observe the present moment as it is, without judgement or a need to change it in any way. That full surrendering to the moment, as it is, is an effortless contrast to the state of striving that we often find ourselves in. Mindfulness invites us to experience the life that is happening right now, not somewhere else in some other time. Perhaps most importantly, it will bring us back to our true nature.

# Reacting or responding to life is your 'response-ability'

When you begin to be more present in life, you become aware of what you yourself bring to the moment you are in. You notice the state of being that you are in. You notice what you are thinking and feeling, and the reactions and choices that subsequently arise. You will begin to realize that you have a choice in how you respond to what is happening in the moment, as it is unfolding. The single-breath practice from #hack 3 can be enough to open up a gap between stimuli and your response. When you are present in that gap, your response to what is unfolding in life will begin to change, and so will your life as a result. Before long you start to own every thought, word, choice and action you take. You realize you are choosing them all. In doing so, you can't help but start to gravitate towards better choices.

When I first began practising mindfulness meditation in the late 1990s, I started to develop a new level of self-awareness. At that time, I was very driven and goal orientated. What I hadn't noticed, until developing increased awareness, was the impact I had on others while achieving my goals. Like anyone else, I didn't set out to be inconsiderate of people's feelings and efforts; in fact, quite the opposite. However, when I paid more attention, I found I could be thoughtless to those around me, albeit unintentionally. I observed myself to be quite selfish and ungrateful at times, all in the name of being driven.

I can share with you that the whole process of becoming more self-aware can be a humbling experience. *Ignorance is bliss* comes to mind. It's far easier to blame other people or things for anything wrong in life, or to put it down to bad luck or stress. It is quite something to realize that the common denominator in it all is us. I am not going to lie – there are some dark nights of the ego along the journey of developing self-awareness. They are, however, to be welcomed because they offer much growth and wisdom. I often tell people that meditation, and the ability to be fully present, have completely changed my life and they continue to do so today. I am so grateful that these practices continue to free me from fear and move me further into peace, love and joy. With just one conscious breath I can always find the steadiness amid any of my chaos. Peace, love and joy sound such a cliché, but the more I learn to be fully present in the moment, the more I experience them.

## Choosing the direction of your focus

The starting point of both self-awareness and mindfulness is a genuine desire to be more present in this moment. When you start to bring your awareness to the present moment, you will likely become aware of just how often your focus is not here. You might find that your attention span is short and that your focus and thoughts jump about all over the place. If you can even notice that that is happening, you are somewhat present.

Our thoughts are often in the past or the future – whether they are of a neutral, positive or negative nature. When in the past, thoughts may be dwelling on something that happened earlier in the day or they might be about an event that occurred a considerable time ago. Likewise, when in the future, thoughts might be on something coming up later in the day or an event sometime in the future.

Thoughts might be about other people within the past and future tense. With our growing addiction to smartphones, it's also likely that we're wondering whether we should check in with social media to see what everyone is doing. At times we might notice we have zoned out completely. All of these variations take us out of being fully present in this moment. All of these are perfectly normal and we don't need to try to stop them happening. Through doing mindfulness practices they will naturally start to dissipate as a side-effect of the practice.

## How to begin a mindfulness practice – breath awareness

I have already mentioned the single-breath practice as a great way to bring yourself into the present moment, and I highly recommend using it in your everyday life.

To start a mindfulness practice right now though, have a go by paying attention to five breaths. To begin… sit comfortably and when you are ready, close your eyes and bring your focus to your breath, simply noticing your inhale and exhale for five breaths.

It is likely that despite your effort to keep your focus on your breath, your mind drifts into other thoughts or zones out. *Notice when this happens*; that is part of the practice. As and when it does happen, simply invite your focus back to the breath. There is no need to judge or become attached to thoughts, feelings or distractions – you are just trying to notice that they are arising. Let them come and go, and come back to observing the breath.

I highly recommend doing this breath practice every day. Start with five breaths, then build up to ten or 20 minutes.

Less is more. Frequency is key. Daily practice of intentionally staying focused on five breaths is better than 20 minutes of going through the motions every now and then.

People sometimes find it frustrating to become aware of just how busy and out of control their mind is. Because they find the practice challenging, they judge that 'they are no good at it' and have the urge to give up. I would encourage you to be patient with yourself and know that, like all things, practice develops skill and ability.

In addition to the breath practice you have just done, there are many breath practices and mindfulness apps available. I recommend the Headspace app as a great resource and starting point.[5] You will also find practices on my website, www.louiselloyd.life. In any case, it's worth the effort of finding a resource that works for you.

Remember, mindfulness is not about stopping thoughts; it's about observing what is, as it is. If that means that you observe that you are having a lot of thoughts then you are still practising mindfulness. What you are trying to do is to *intentionally* choose to be present enough to notice. Over time, the ability of being able to choose your focus, and remain non-attached to and non-judgemental of anything that arises, will bring you more peace and ease than you can imagine.

I will cover more of this later in the book. For now though just practise bringing your attention to the present moment. Have enough awareness to notice what you yourself are bringing to the moment. Notice your internal physical, mental and emotional state of being and the choice and actions you are making as a result of these.

---

[5] For information on the Headspace app, see www.headspace.com

# The hack

Use the single-breath practice to bring your focus and attention into the present moment. Be open to observing the present moment, exactly as it is, in a non-judgemental way. It is what it is.

Notice what you bring to the present moment. Notice your state of being. Living mindfully requires you to notice your thoughts, your feelings and the options and actions you are choosing.

# LIVE AND LET LIVE

When you start to become more present and begin to notice your thoughts, you will likely notice how judgemental many of them are. We have a personal story running through just about everything. We all see the world through the lens of our own past experiences and resulting opinions, so our perception of reality will often be different to someone else's.

In any given moment, there are at least two versions of reality. There is the actual reality, as it happens neutrally; and the reality we see through our own lens. If somebody pushes in front of you in a queue to buy some water, it would be easy to think that the person is rude and that they have no right to push in. You might feel enraged by what they have just done. If the reality of the situation is that somebody had just fainted outside of the shop and the person was trying to help as quickly as they could, then you would likely be very happy to let them through. At that moment, they might not have had time to explain what they were doing, and they may well have appeared rude. Recognizing this helps us to realize that our perceptions of reality are often limited and flawed. That person might have appeared impatient and rude at the time, but it doesn't mean that *they* are rude and impatient.

Likewise, we can pre-judge a future moment. Let's say you have a meeting next week with someone that you don't like. It is likely that you have pre-judged that the meeting will be awful, and you are already dreading it. It might be a fact that you don't like the person and that you find them challenging. In pre-judging the experience of the meeting though, you haven't allowed for the possibility that the *actual* meeting could be perfectly OK. The person might be quite reasonable on that occasion, and the meeting could go well.

In pre-judging, you add an unnecessary layer of suffering to your life. Though you are not in the meeting yet, you are already feeling uneasy about it; even though that unease may be unfounded. Even if the meeting is awful, you don't need to experience it until the actual time you are in it. You could choose to remain open-minded and wait and see what happens.

Stress can often bring us to limited dualistic thinking, and when it does, we become more judgemental. Using the single-breath practice to become more present in each moment will help you to see when you have become dualistic in your thinking and when you are being overly judgemental.

## How do we become less judgemental?

It helps to remind ourselves that how we perceive the present moment is just our version of it, and to recognize that most likely we can't see the full picture.

If we can recognize when we are thinking in duality, we might also observe if we are making a judgement. Good/ bad. Right/wrong. Should/shouldn't. Nice/not nice.

Look out for when you are making a judgement about someone else's behaviour. You do not know the reasons behind what they do/don't do, unless you ask them. We really don't need to have an opinion about what everyone is or isn't doing and why they might be doing or not doing it. As it turns out, quite a lot in life doesn't need to be any of our business. It was also quite a revelation to me to drop needing to have to have an opinion about everything. I have found considerable peace from realizing that I can say that 'I have no idea' and to not need to have one! Far from that showing indifference, it has allowed me the openness to let life unfold and reveal itself exactly as it is, without needing to have an opinion or judgement about it. I can highly recommend it – but then that's just my opinion!

## # The hack

Breathe. Get present. If you are present you will notice when you are being unnecessarily judgemental or opinionated.

Notice that when you are getting stressed about a future event, then you have already pre-judged how it will turn out. Remind yourself that you are not there yet and that the event might not be how you are pre-judging it to be.

Recognize that your opinions and judgements are a result of your own life experience, and may or may not be clouding your perception of the current reality.

Notice if you are overthinking anyone else's business and behaviour. Do you need to? What purpose does it serve?

# IT IS WHAT IT IS

In life's challenging moments, it can be difficult to accept the moment as it is. In the wise, and often repeated, words of the Borg from *Star Trek*, 'resistance is futile'. There really is no point in resisting reality. Accepting the moment as it is doesn't mean we accept anything and everything in our life without having any control over it. It means that we are not in resistance to the very moment we are in. Being in resistance adds unnecessary suffering to that which already is.

An example of this is being stuck in traffic. You can wish you weren't and get frustrated that you are, but this will cause unnecessary suffering and won't make the traffic disappear. On the other hand, if you accept that you are stuck in traffic, your journey will be a more peaceful one. It might be a choice to find a different route, but you can still accept that there is traffic. You don't have to get stressed about it.

You might be thinking that it's all well and good other than when you will be late for something important. I agree. However, if there is traffic, even though you don't want to be late, the traffic is something that is out of your control, so you're going to be late whether you like it or not. What is in your control is whether you turn up in a calm or flustered state when you eventually get there, albeit late.

The concept of accepting the moment as it is confuses some people. They think it means that if you are in a situation that isn't OK then you just keep going along with it. This is not what acceptance means. It doesn't mean that we don't respond to life – we still do, just more consciously. We just stop resisting that which we cannot change. Often we find ourselves in resistance to these moments because we would rather they were different. Of course, there are many moments we would likely prefer were different; it just serves no purpose to waste energy wishing they were. Instead, we respond to life exactly as it is, without being in resistance to it.

You may like or dislike any moment you find yourself in. But the moment you accept it as it is, irrelevant of how it is, you free yourself up to bring your conscious awareness to it and to own your response. You will also significantly reduce your stress.

I find applying this to things I am procrastinating over also helps. There are chores or situations we just have to deal with that we might prefer not to – perhaps it's a part of our job that we find a bit dull or that we don't like flying but we want to go on holiday. The moment we accept them as they are, along with the fact that we don't have to enjoy them, it somehow frees us up to just get on and do them. We stop wasting energy in putting them off, or dreading them. We just get on with it. It is what it is. They are what they are.

# # The hack

Every time you find yourself in resistance to the moment you are in, breathe.

Say to yourself: 'It is what it is. I don't have to like it.'

Ask yourself: 'What's in my control right now? What isn't?'

Ask yourself: 'Accepting this moment as it is, how do I want to respond to it?'

# ALL CHANGE

Change and uncertainty can be a major cause of stress, especially when we haven't chosen it. Whether it's a major change coming out of the blue, or the frequency and speed that projects keep changing at work, change can unnerve and frustrate us. In the technological world that we now live in, change occurs more frequently and quicker than ever before. There is no point resisting that fact so we may as well learn to adapt.

#Hack 23 covered accepting the moment as it is, and accepting change is no different. If something or someone has or is changing then this is how it is, whether we like it or not. What we can do is equip ourselves to handle change. We can still choose how we respond to it. While change can take some acclimatizing to, it also has many benefits and opportunities.

In a classic Kubler-Ross Change Curve,[6] we might go through a range of emotions. If we haven't seen change coming, we might experience a feeling of shock. This could trigger us into denial and bargaining while we try to understand what's going on and why. We may go through

---

[6] E. Kubler-Ross, *On death and dying*, 1969. The Kubler-Ross Change Curve is also known as the Grief Curve.

waves of anger and frustration, grief and sadness. We might wish to escape the whole thing as we keep bouncing from one emotion to the other. At some point, if we can reach a state of acceptance, we will start to explore the new reality, often through considerable trial and error, until we start to create and co-operate with the pathway ahead.

Not all of us experience all of these emotions when we face change, and it will largely depend on the circumstances of how and what has changed. We might experience a degree of frustration and bargaining when projects keep changing at work. And we would be very likely to experience a lengthy and extremely challenging range of emotions if we are going through divorce or bereavement. In any case, trying to find our way to acceptance will reduce our suffering as much as possible.

To reduce stress as you navigate change:

- Honour how you feel. You are a normal human being, with normal human emotions and you are very likely to experience a whole range of them during times of change.
- Try to come to an acceptance of what is changing or has changed. That may take time but keep in mind that at some point it is better for you to reach a state of acceptance than not to.
- Breathe. More than ever, the breath practices will help to settle your over-reactive nervous system.
- Watch your inner storylines. Apply #hack 29 to stop your overthinking running off with you.
- Be patient. With yourself. With other people. With the process. New habits and new circumstances all take time to become more comfortable with. It's all trial and error, and that is perfectly OK.

- Look after your own wellbeing. More of that in Part 6.
- Trust yourself. Mostly we fear change because we fear that we might not cope. Remember, when there is a gap between where you are and the challenge you face, identify what is needed to close that gap.
- It's good to talk. Yep, more than ever, during change there will likely be some awkward conversations to navigate but they are definitely worth having.
- Look for the positive through all change. Ask yourself: 'What can I learn from this?'
- Own every moment of your response to change. That's the bit you get to do something about. Keep bringing your focus into the moment you are in and doing what you can, with what you have, and where you are.

## # The hack

Recognize where you are in the change curve. What emotions are you experiencing?

What's in your control? What isn't?

Own your response to change. What can you do? What do you need?

Look out for your storylines. Change and uncertainty doesn't need to be negative – it depends how we frame it.

If you are struggling with change, know that all things pass.

Breathe! One moment at a time.

Keep bringing your focus into the moment you are in and doing what you can, with what you have, and where you are.

# WHAT'S DONE IS DONE

There are two ways of dealing with the past. We can hang on to it, which can't help but hold us back from fully experiencing life as it unfolds in the present; or we can learn from it and choose to be in a continual state of release, accepting all that has gone before us. We can learn from all experiences – the joyful, the painful and all else in between. It doesn't all need to be pretty. It highly likely won't be.

Whether it is the past that occurred just a moment ago, or from many years ago, we always have the option of acknowledging what can be learnt and then finding the courage to be open to what the future might bring. Nobody can release our past for us – only we can do that, in the best way for us. Sometimes it takes years to come to an acceptance of a painful past, but never lose sight that acceptance frees us up for the future. Every single day is an opportunity to start over. To begin again. To choose what we bring to this moment.

I can only offer a few of my own personal tips for how I myself try to be at peace with the past. I encourage you to find your own way to come to peace with anything from your past too. As Nelson Mandela famously said when he was released from prison after 27 years:

As I walked out of the door toward the gate that would lead to my freedom, I knew that if I didn't leave my bitterness and hatred behind, I'd still be in prison.

We all hold our own keys to releasing our past, even if that's not easy.

Here are a few suggestions to help come to peace with the past, be that in the short term or long term:

- Accept that whatever happened in the past isn't happening in this moment right now.
- Learn from the mistakes you have made and the things that you have done that, in hindsight, you wouldn't repeat. Apologize to anyone concerned if it's needed. Forgive yourself, and then draw a line under it. Move on. Live and learn.
- When you have experienced pain as a result of the choices or actions of others, acknowledge the pain that you have felt. Also acknowledge that because you love and care for yourself, you do not want to carry that pain any longer than it takes to release it.
- As best you can, try to have humility and understanding that we all make mistakes and will all cause pain to others, mostly unintentionally. We are all doing the best that we can, even when it appears the exact opposite.
- Seek out whatever professional help you might need for anything that holds you back as a result of the past.
- Know that the past cannot be released until you decide that you are willing to do this.

- Take one day at a time.
- Use the single-breath practice in #hack 3 to keep bringing yourself into the present moment. You are not in your past any more; you just need reminding sometimes.
- Look at the positives you can take from the past. I have learnt some of the best life lessons from the most painful parts of my past. They have taught me compassion, understanding and patience. They have taught me that I have the strength to overcome my worst fears. I have also learnt the humility that we are all capable of causing another pain, and of being on the receiving end of pain. I also know that we can get through it and that there are people to help us to do so.
- Know that we will continue to live and learn our entire lives. We will always have the potential to be a better person today than the one we were yesterday. The choice of doing that lies entirely in our hands.

## # The hack

If your past is holding you back in any way, do whatever you need to do to come to peace with it, to learn from it and to move on. Find a way.

Accept that we will continue to have the opportunity to learn for our entire lives, so we can always be open to the wisdom that can only come from life's experiences, both the joyful and the painful.

Use the single-breath practice from #hack 3 to keep bringing yourself into the present moment. You are no longer in your past. You are in this moment. Every single moment is an invitation to start over, again and again.

# LOOSENING THE GRIP ON THE FUTURE

Let me be honest – none of us have a clue what our future holds in store for us. Sure, we can do our best to visualize it, plan it, steer it and wish for it; but in the end it will be what it will be.

The more we try to predict and control it, the tighter we become and the more anxiety we feel. If we take a step back, we can see that all of our anxiety arises from our desire to control what isn't in our control. Despite our desire to have a guarantee, we will never have one, and that's OK. Despite our desire to have all of the answers, we don't need to. That would limit us from evolving and take away our freedom to respond to an ever-unfolding adventure.

If we trusted that we could cope with whatever life brings our way, we wouldn't live in fear of it. If we knew that we could equip ourselves to face whatever we needed to face, then we would worry less about doing so. If we believed that there was a grand plan in action that on some level we are co-creating, we would learn to go with the flow. If we could learn to balance any future plans and goals with living in the moment we are in, we would find that life unfolded in a much more enjoyable way.

Much of our fear around the future is that we are terrified of making *wrong* choices. But what if we were to consider that every choice we make leads us to exactly the point that serves us best? If we recognized that we are constantly responding to life and can choose to change direction at any given moment? We can't get it wrong. Ever. We are always choosing to have the experiences that we will learn from, whether we know it or not. We can learn to trust ourselves to meet life as it arrives and we can always equip ourselves with what we need.

The irony about securing the best possible future for ourselves is that if we bring our full awareness to each moment, as we live it, we will continue to be in tune with what's in our best interest. We have an in-built sat-nav that guides our best choices, if we find the time and stillness to listen to it. If we live now; not in the future.

Some of us like more longer-term plans than others do. Whichever camp you are in, just allow a little elbow room for your plans to change. When I was growing up, I was 100% certain that I wanted to be an Olympic event rider. I spent the best part of 20 years pouring my entire life into following that dream, until the day I fell out of love with it and changed course completely. If you had said to me when I was competing that I would choose to give up and go on to a career that gave me even more joy and fulfilment, I would have laughed at you. It was impossible! Except that it wasn't, and I have.

You see, we all change, and our futures will unfold for us as we do. We live in a world where so much is possible. We can research and learn anything we want to at the touch of our fingertips. Even when life throws a curve-ball into our futures, we have so many ways of overcoming all that we face. We can't get it wrong.

So, if you do get stressed about the future, take a reality check. Try these tips:

- Plan and choose your path as best you can now, with the knowledge and experience you have. Get advice from whoever you need to help with that. Nothing needs to be set in stone. Everything you decide to choose now is the best for you.
- Use the single-breath practice to bring yourself into the present moment any time you are getting too swept up in worrying about the future. You are not in it yet. You are wherever you are right now, that's all.
- Give your present life your all, whatever it looks like.
- Know that you always have options. Remember the change it/accept it/leave it choice of response you have.
- Use longer breath practices and whatever other relaxation techniques you find helpful to keep soothing your nervous system.
- Take life one day at a time, one choice at a time.
- If you don't like the path you are currently following, change it! If you feel totally stuck in life, repeat #hack 1 as often as you need to. Then see what the next step is after that. One step at a time.
- Know that just because you feel anxious about the future, it doesn't mean your future will be anything worthy of worrying about.

- Trust that all things work out as they are meant to. There are no coincidences. If you want more evidence of this, read Michael Singer's book *The Surrender Experiment*.[7] His entire life is a living example of how miraculous going with the flow can be.

---

## # The hack

Accept the reality that none of us have a clue what our future holds in store for us. And that is OK. Balance future plans with bringing your focus and energy into living in the present moment.

Breathe; take one day at a time. You can always equip yourself to face whatever the future brings. Know that just because you feel anxious about the future, it doesn't mean that your future is something to fear – that's just the story you are telling yourself.

---

[7]   M. Singer, *The surrender experiment*, 2015.

# THANK YOU!

Stress can blinker us from noticing all the good things in life. We get so wrapped up in our head that we fail to notice the beauty of the simple things that surround us. We stop noticing the love and care that our loved ones wrap our days in. We stop noticing the taste of our food, the appearance of a blue sky or a smile on someone's face. We stop noticing most things, other than the things that stress us out. In doing so, we forget how lucky we really are.

When we are stressed, things get out of perspective. A bad day probably isn't a bad day; it's more likely a single isolated event that you've ruminated over all day. You will have totally missed all the good things that happened because you have viewed them through the lens of that one isolated event. We focus on all that is wrong and miss all that is right.

When we are stressed, we take so many things for granted. We focus on all the things we haven't got, and forget about the things we already have. We don't appreciate how lucky we are simply to have a roof over our head, a bed to sleep in and food to eat.

Learning to be more present in each moment will help you to notice the good things that surround you. You will notice that even the most normal, random day is filled with

103

things to be grateful for. You will realize the joy that can be found from the simple things in life – like hearing the birds sing, having a cup of tea, or enjoying the comfort of your bed. You will feel enriched by a beautiful moment spent with loved ones rather than taking them for granted. You will enjoy time spent putting your kids to bed, rather than your mind being on all the things you have to do. Everyday life becomes less going through the motions and more alive.

When you start to pay attention to these moments, you start to notice more and more of them. You start feeling grateful for so much in your life, and that in and of itself feels amazing. Have you ever noticed how good it feels to come home after you've been away? Or how good a glass of water tastes when you are extremely thirsty?

Practising an attitude of gratitude really is good for your stress levels, but you do need to be realistic about where you start. It's not about faking it. It's about looking out for things that you can genuinely be grateful for and, depending on your stress levels, that might take some effort to identify. I promise you that it's worth it.

So, what in your life can you be grateful for, right now? Who are you grateful for?

If you were to spend an entire week with the sole purpose of looking out for things to be grateful for, you couldn't help but feel your life being enriched. Your stress levels would drop as a side-effect and you would remember what it feels like to feel good about life. Of all of the hacks in this book, there are some that I personally feel are game-changers – this is one of them.

Having an attitude of gratitude is multi-layered and starts to create an upturn of events in your life. When you begin to feel more gratitude in everyday life, you will inevitably start to be more generous with others. And that too feels amazing. It's in the giving that we receive and all that – turns out that it's true. If you get stressed in your car journey to and from work and want to turn it into a more positive experience, try going out of your way to be generous to other drivers. Let drivers out at junctions; be generous in your patience with a slow driver or with someone that cuts you up because they too are totally stressed out in life. Drive a tad slower than you usually do; let lorry drivers out on dual carriageways. Try it, as an experiment. It might add a few minutes to your journey but it also might change your whole day.

Look for as many ways as you can to be generous with others. Be patient with a work colleague. Put loose change into a charity box. Hold a door open for someone. Get someone a coffee. Whatever works for you – when you start looking for opportunities to be generous with others, you will see an abundance of them.

When you start to be more generous in your everyday life, generosity can't help but start coming towards you at every turn. It really is a win-win. You feel great when you give to others and you feel grateful for everything that the world is giving to you.

Honestly, don't take my word for it. I'm saying it's a total game-changer, but you won't notice any of these benefits in your own life if you don't practise it. Here's the flip – mostly we are grateful and generous when things are going really well in life. You need to do it now, even if life sucks. Then see just how easily life starts to change.

# # The hack

For a whole week, look out for things to be grateful for. Set it as an absolute intention that wherever you go, whatever you are doing, you are on the lookout for things to appreciate.

For the following week, go out of your way to be generous to others, in whatever form that takes. Opportunities to be generous are everywhere. Don't seek or expect anything in return. Just give.

Why a whole week? Because if you make the effort to focus on both of these points for a week at a time, you will want to be grateful and generous forever.

*Part 5*

# BEING YOU

You are totally unique. As am I. And everyone else too.

We all have our talents, and we all have our struggles. In Part 5 you will learn to be less your own-worst-enemy-self and more your own-best-friend-self. You will gain the tools to help you to quieten down your overthinking mind, face your fears and get comfortable outside of your comfort zone. You'll be equipped to move beyond all that gets in the way of you bringing your gifts and talents into the world, and you will learn to love being you while you do it. When you learn to become your own-best-friend-self there will be no stopping you!

And all of this starts with you saying to yourself these five words…

## *It's OK to be me…*

# BE YOU!

Yes! There are approximately 7.5 billion people in the world, and we are all unique. How exciting is that! There is so much contrast and variation in absolutely everything, including us. We can all have unique gifts and talents. We don't need to agree on everything. We can like and dislike different things. We can be brilliant at some things and totally useless at others. My pappa had a brilliant way of explaining things and would often say, 'it's the same but different'. We're like that as people – the same but different.

I value honesty, authenticity, love, faith and courage. I am loving, caring and hard-working. I can be over-emotional, defensive and insecure. I love nature, the sea, mountains, champagne, romance, skiing, golf, modern open-plan houses, beautiful gardens, wine, vegetables and salad. I love having a flexible diary, the work that I do, helping people and having deep, philosophical conversation.

I don't like noisy or overcrowded spaces, clutter, sweet drinks or meat. I enjoy walking and yoga, not the gym. I have no problem standing up to speak in front of hundreds of people but I am mostly quite introverted. I am a morning person. I like being around people, and I need my own space. I love working for myself and would hate a nine-to-five job. These are just a few of the details that make up who I am at the moment and, of course, these could all change.

Who are you right now? What are your preferences? What do you like? Dislike? What works for you? What doesn't?

Don't waste any more time being anyone else but you. Give yourself full permission to be who you are, as you are. Accept even the bits that you want to change.

Don't waste any more time thinking that you're not enough either. I mean that.

You totally are enough. You are a unique individual that has been put on this earth for a reason. It isn't a coincidence. You are not just here for the sake of being here; you are here to be you.

You were born into this world with a unique blend of gifts, talents, potential and purpose, along with some unique, personal challenges to overcome.

Exactly as you are, right now, is exactly how you are meant to be. You are becoming more self-aware and you are going to look after your needs. You are going to look after yourself enough so that you can be who you have come here to be.

You know that, at heart, you are kind, generous, gifted and have an inherent desire to love and be loved. You also have a brilliant blend of individual quirks and uniqueness. We all do. We're all the same, but oh so amazingly different too.

# # The hack

Give yourself permission to be you, exactly as you are. Love your uniqueness, even if not everyone does. Be your talents, and enjoy them. Don't be ashamed of your fears and insecurities but work to overcome them.

Drop all pressure to be anyone other than the person you are and the one you are choosing to become. That's the point of self-development – you are becoming an evolved version of yourself. You are not trying to become someone else. What a waste that would be!

# DON'T FALL FOR YOUR OVERTHINKING

Honestly, don't fall for your overthinking – it is just a whole lot of inner noise. In an attempt to gain understanding and control over that which we fear, we start to overthink. Before we know it, our incessant overthinking won't leave us alone. This especially happens when we feel left in the dark about something that we find stressful or upsetting. We start filling in the blanks and, though we have no idea whether we are right or not, we do it anyway. We can go from a slight concern to full-blown catastrophic thinking in the blink of an eye. This is another symptom of a nervous system on high alert. Our mind becomes suspicious of everything. We go into overdrive trying to work out what we can trust and what we can't. The problem with feeling like everything is a potential threat is that it isn't long before we see everyone as a potential enemy.

If we were to step back from it all, we would see the craziness of our irrational thoughts. When totally consumed by them, we only see the world through the lens of our fears and worries. Rational thinking seems to have disappeared. At times of stress we are thinking from the survival part of our brain, which thinks in dualistic terms: fight or run.

We see things as black or white; friend or enemy; right or wrong; all or nothing; my way or the highway. We close off so much potential and we stay trapped in the cycle of negative and limiting thinking.

Next time you are overthinking, try this:

1. Breathe! I cannot stress highly enough (sorry, no pun intended) how important it is to steady yourself in the breath. Remember, it triggers the relaxation response and will help you to feel less anxious, which in and of itself will reduce your overthinking tendencies.

2. Remind yourself that most of the inner storylines you have running probably aren't true. You can stop them in their tracks by catching yourself as you are thinking them, and ask yourself: 'Do I know this is a fact?' Check out the work of Byron Katie, who explores this concept further in her brilliant work on stressful thoughts.[8]

3. When you are playing out a worst-case scenario in your mind, ask yourself: 'What other possible outcomes might there be?'

4. Remind yourself what's in your control, and try to accept what isn't.

5. Refer back to #hack 11 in addressing whatever it is you are overthinking.

6. Every time you notice that your mind has wandered into overthinking, use the single-breath practice (see #hack 3) and ask yourself what you would rather be thinking about/doing right now. Bring your focus

---

[8] See http://thework.com

to what you want to think about or do, and keep doing so every time you notice you've slipped into overthinking again. If you keep choosing to do this, your ability to do so will increase. Be patient with yourself. In the early stages of trying this you might find it challenging to shift focus, but keep trying – it will get better.

7. Remind yourself that you are doing the best that you can, and all things work out one way or another. Sometimes we don't always see that there can be a bigger picture at play than the one we see. In hindsight we will always see this.

## # The hack

To calm an overthinking mind, breathe! Remind yourself what's in your control and accept what isn't. Stop every wayward thought in its tracks by asking yourself: 'Do I know this is a fact?'

Recognize that you are doing the best that you can and that all things work out one way or another. In hindsight, we will always see this. Say to yourself: 'I trust that all things work out for the best, even when I can't see it'.

# FACING FEAR

Fear, in and of itself, is not the enemy. But the relationship we have with it can be.

Fear has helped to keep us alive. It warns us of threat. Rarely though are we in the danger that our nervous system is designed to react to. It is reacting to things that serve no real threat at all. That's why our heart pounds through our chest when we are outside of our comfort zone. We don't feel safe when, in reality, we are. Though we might dread walking into a room full of strangers, for example, it isn't actually going to kill us. We know that, but our triggered response feels otherwise. That's where the breath practices really do help because they calm the nervous system down enough for us to regain perspective.

Despite the physiological symptoms we feel when we are fearful, we don't have to be stopped by them. We can learn how to navigate them and keep them in perspective. When I used to compete, I found it very helpful to keep things in perspective. If I was nervous warming up at a competition, I would tell myself that as much as this event feels massive to me now, tomorrow it will all be history. Whether I win, lose or totally mess up – by tomorrow it will be done. Oddly, reframing it that way enabled me to focus and get on with the task at hand, which was doing the best I could on that day – whatever the result.

Some of the other competitors would actually be physically sick from nerves before they competed. Even though they might have been Olympic gold medallists, they still felt nerves – and it didn't get in the way of them winning. They learnt to feel the fear and do it anyway, so to speak (as Susan Jeffers covers in her book, *Feel the Fear and Do It Anyway: How to Turn Your Fear and Indecision into Confidence and Action*).[9] As much as that is a cliché, it highlights that it isn't so much the fear itself that is the issue, more how we choose to respond when we feel it.

It can be helpful to remind ourselves that all feelings pass and that we are not alone in feeling them. As uncomfortable as you might feel leading up to and giving a presentation, those feelings will pass, as will the presentation. They won't kill you. I know that you know that, and that you only get so nervous because you want it to go well. But if you really care about it going well then you will choose to learn how to ride the discomfort that you feel.

When you feel your heart racing, have a dry mouth or you are trembling, you don't need to attach to those sensations at all. You can just notice them, breathe and let them be there. Once we understand this, feeling fear can even become a game. We can play with the edges of our fear when it surfaces, and begin to reframe it as excitement and eager anticipation. It can make us feel amazingly alert and alive, and we can become comfortable being uncomfortable.

---

[9] S. Jeffers, *Feel the fear and do it anyway: How to turn your fear and indecision into confidence and action*, 2007.

Fear around the future because of past experience, like the fear you might feel about having a new relationship after your previous partner left you, or driving after an accident, or the fear of a cancer returning, is perfectly natural to feel. The same loss of perspective and worst-case-scenario storylines are likely to be prevalent. The breath practices, talking to friends, taking each day as it comes can all help you to navigate these sorts of fears. As will being loving and patient with yourself. You are doing the best that you can, always. However intense the fear is, recognize that you are not your fear.

Look out for your fight-or-flight reactiveness (see #hack 9) and remember that when triggered in fear, you will likely lose all rational thinking and become completely over-reactive and over-sensitive. It's OK. Breathe. Continuing to address your fear (also see #hack 11 for addressing the cause of stress) in a proactive way will help you to not only navigate it when it arises, but will also help you to move through it and beyond it.

I have learnt that the only lasting way to deal with fear is not to avoid it. To sit with it, without trying to change it, run from it or get rid of it. Simply to breathe through it. When you have the confidence to sit with your fears, you will likely have three life-changing realizations: 1) You are not your fear. 2) You can get comfortable with it. And 3) It doesn't have to stop you doing anything.

Feeling fear is a normal part of being human. Learning to navigate fear is self-mastery, and the beginning of a far better life.

# The hack

Recognize that fear is not the enemy. It is possible to get comfortable with fear and to navigate the physiological response to it. Breathe. Breathe. Breathe. Don't attach meaning to the physiological response, other than it is your nervous system reacting to a threat that isn't really a threat. Unless, of course, you really are under threat and then you need to react to it! Use #hack 9 and #hack 11 to address fear.

# LIFE OUTSIDE OF YOUR COMFORT ZONE

There are many things in life that take us out of our comfort zone. Sometimes we are just momentarily outside of it due to something trivial, like bumping into someone we'd rather not see, or feeling unprepared for a meeting. Other times, it's when we are facing a significant challenge and we are way beyond the boundaries of comfort, perhaps like becoming a parent for the first time or looking for a new job after being made redundant. Different situations are uncomfortable for different people.

What does being outside of our comfort zone feel like?

Well, obviously, it feels uncomfortable. Perhaps it's a feeling of vulnerability. Of being out of our depth. Out on a limb. Out of control. Or when we feel on the edges of, or beyond, our current skillset. Feeling unsure. Nervous, perhaps. Times when we might question our ability. Maybe we wonder if we are doing the right thing. It can feel like being under a spotlight – exposing all of our weaknesses. Mostly there is fear, albeit that it might be disguised as something else.

Personally, I am often way outside of my comfort zone. We all are. I have learnt not to let being outside of my comfort zone get in my way. I have learnt, and continue to learn, to surf the wave of discomfort rather than let it drown me. There are many times I am beyond my comfort zone but I have learnt to breathe through it. You can do the same.

So, when do you feel outside of your comfort zone?

Is it standing up in front of people to speak? Sharing how you feel with others? Moving on from heartbreak? Applying for a promotion or new job? Having an awkward conversation? Walking into a room full of strangers? Picking yourself back up from a disappointment? Being ill? Feeling mental, emotional or physical pain? Getting fit? Being asked to solve a problem that you don't know the answer to?

We don't have to look too far to find the boundaries of our individual comfort zones. Or to identify the situations that we try to avoid. The things that we put off doing. The stuff that we dread or that we delay because it's not the right time.

Not having enough time can be a perfect excuse for all those outside of our comfort-zone situations. Sometimes we have a choice to avoid being in such circumstances, but often we don't. Often life takes us right into that space whether we like it or not.

The question is: how do we learn to ride that wave of discomfort if we want to? How do we equip ourselves with the confidence to lean into these moments? Without doubt, these are the moments that can offer growth and expansion, or cause us to contract and withdraw.

Exploring life outside of our comfort zone has the potential to move us past self-imposed limitations. Learning to navigate that uncomfortable space is life-changing. It gives us freedom from that which we fear. It isn't about finding the absence of fear; more that we learn to master feeling it.

Oddly, if we can just shift our mindset to being there, being in that uncomfortable space can become comfortable. It can be revealing; a playground of enquiry. Strangely, it can be exciting and fulfilling. Not always. If we are way outside of our comfort zone because we are going through something traumatic, it doesn't feel exciting at all. It feels horrific. So, at times like this, of course we would rather not be in it, but we learn how to be. We learn how to be present in that space, even though fear and pain would push us to do otherwise.

## How?

Firstly, by bravely choosing to be present in it. By learning to steady ourselves in our breath. As we have already covered, the breath gives space between how we feel and how we react. When we are outside of our comfort zone there are often in-your-face physiological symptoms that are far from joyful. Our heart might be pounding. Our breathing erratic. Loss of focus. Overwhelming fear. All of the above and more. But if you choose to breathe through it all, it won't stop you.

The breath is a game-changer. It slows things down, enables rational thinking, moves us beyond fight, flight or freeze. We can see the bigger picture and clarify what we are trying to achieve. Once we can do that, we can better navigate our way through it. Does it mean we will feel entirely comfortable? No, not always – but more often than you would think.

When we feel out of our comfort zone, it is often because we feel a discrepancy between what we want to achieve and our belief in being able to do so. Remember – that's the gap that we feel when stressed. If we can identify what we need to do to reach the higher goal of the situation, it can help us to move through it. We can nudge our way, one manageable step at a time, towards our goal. It helps to identify the bigger *why*.

When we can think of the higher meaning of why we are trying to achieve something, it helps us to ride out the inner fears we experience when we are outside of our comfort zone. It helps us to move through them for some purpose bigger than us; something that is more important than our fear. For example, when people are raising money for a charity, they often find the inner strength to push themselves way beyond their comfortable limits. When there is a higher purpose, courage and strength will find us if we are willing.

People often feel out of their comfort zone when faced with projects that appear insurmountable. Take writing this book as an example. For quite some time, I had wanted to do it to support the work that I do. As I have never written a book before, the whole process of getting content onto paper and how to go through the publishing process felt quite overwhelming to me. When I started to look into it all, I realized what a significant undertaking it would be. I procrastinated, starting the odd page here and there before delaying because I 'wasn't in the right headspace'. All sorts of convenient reasons surfaced as to why I wasn't getting on with writing the book.

To clear this block, I took a step back and asked myself what my motivation was for writing it, and what fear was stopping me. I identified that my motivation was to help people feel less stressed and to help them to be the amazing people they are capable of being. Then I asked myself how I would define whether it would be worth putting all the time and expense into writing the book. I decided that if the book helped even just a few people, then it would be worth it.

As for the fears that were stopping me getting on with it – oh, yes, I have been way outside of my comfort zone. Fear of what people would think of me writing a book, let alone what they would think if they actually read it. Fear of there already being so many great books out there. Fear of spending the thousands of pounds that it would take to publish it. Fear of finding the right publisher. Basically, fear! And a whole lot of unhelpful self-doubt and overthinking to go with it. If I had dwelled too long on those fearful thoughts then I would never have written the book.

To get started, I focused on the people I could help if I wrote it. I broke the process down into doable steps. I researched publishing routes. I read books on how to write books. I drew together a list of content that I thought should be included, and I did a chapter outline.

While I am still massively out of my comfort zone, even now as I write, I have given myself a step-by-step approach and I motivate myself by continually remembering that my goal is to help people. To help you. It helps me to get out of my own way. Knowing that it might reduce your stress or improve the quality of your life helps me to park my own insecurities. I can be comfortable being out of my comfort zone.

You can do the same, whenever you are outside of your comfort zone, for whatever reason. We all just have to choose to reach towards something that is bigger than our fear. We can't lose. We just have to try. And we have to go with it all.

## The long game – step by step

If you signed up for a physical challenge like a marathon, you might well be out of your comfort zone. Throughout the training, you would have days when you didn't feel like putting in the miles, but you would. In the marathon itself, you will likely hit that moment when you don't feel you can run the distance. Let's say it hits at around mile 16 – the thought of running another 10.2 miles might feel impossible.

At moments like that, when you have no idea if you will make it, it can help to come back to the simplicity of only thinking about the one next step. Can you take just this next step? Can you endure the pain you are in just for this next step? That's how we get to any finish line. One single step after another. It's always one moment at a time. One breath after another. It's the same when we are outside of our comfort zone. Can we stay with it just for this moment? How about for the next step?

For many of the situations we find uncomfortable, there isn't an overnight fix to instantly feel comfortable or to achieve our goal. It takes patience, and it takes effort. Know this upfront. See it as a long game. If you look at the commonality between out of your comfort-zone situations, you will see that the same approach works for most of them.

The bottom line is about you managing to sit amid your fears, doubts and discomfort, without them holding you back. It's about being able to do what needs doing now, in this moment. It's about taking this one next step. The ability to do this is something you can practise.

Life, by its very nature, invites us to meet the challenges we face outside of our comfort zone. Being uncomfortable is the signal that we are in that space. That doesn't mean we should back out of it. Rather, it is a sign to get present. To breathe. To lean into the moment by becoming curious about what is required of us and how we can meet it.

We can lovingly invite ourselves to grow into being more than our current self. Every situation is an opportunity to ask 'what can I learn from this?' To ask, 'can I reach just that bit further, just to see where it leads me?' Approached in the right way, being outside of our comfort zone is one of our greatest opportunities, despite often feeling otherwise.

# The hack

Every time you find yourself outside of your comfort zone:

Get present. Breathe.

What's the bigger picture?

What do you need to support yourself?

# CALLING OUT YOUR OWN-WORST-ENEMY-SELF

Here's the thing. At some point, we really do need to stop being our own worst enemy. Well, we do if we want to be happier and less stressed.

Our own worst enemy can sabotage all sorts of things in life, and you can probably recognize your own-worst-enemy-self in action. You might be familiar with that harsh inner critic. At times, this inner critic sits quietly in the background, just putting a dampener on the things you want to get excited about. When you dare to dream, it will remind you of all the reasons your idea is stupid, and of how many times things have gone wrong in the past. It compares you with all the filtered, faked-up versions of anyone else you think is better than you.

And then there's the nagging self-doubt. I don't know many people that don't feel self-doubt at times. Actually, I'm not sure I know any. A bit of self-doubt is healthy; after all, life often invites us outside of our comfort zone and not everything turns out as we want it to. That aside, it's the crippling self-doubt that our own-worst-enemy-self thrives on. We have all suffered disappointments, some more devastating than others. In the fast-paced world that we live in, we don't always allow ourselves time to process the very normal human emotions we go through when things affect us.

But if we don't process those feelings, our own worst enemy will take great pleasure in turning them all in on ourselves. Without even realizing it, we can unconsciously self-sabotage everything that we want and everything that we care about – all to avoid feeling any more potential disappointment or pain. We hold ourselves back and beat ourselves up – and we invest a vast amount of time and energy in doing so. All this at the hands of our very own-worst-enemy-self. It's the villain in our very own Hero's Journey.

But what if we could stop doing that? What if we could actually encourage and support ourselves in life?

Somehow, we need to learn to be our own-best-friend-self. We need to start supporting and encouraging ourselves just like a best friend would. We need to give ourselves a chance in life.

## It's OK – I hear you

The first step in becoming your own-best-friend-self is to make time to listen to your own-worst-enemy-self and to hear all of its fears. Why? Because, as self-sabotaging as your own-worst-enemy-self is, it's only trying to stop you getting hurt. It thinks it's got your best interests at heart, even though it doesn't.

So, before you go any further, go and get yourself a pen and plenty of paper. Make yourself a cuppa, and maybe get a box of tissues, and go shut yourself in a room somewhere quiet and comfortable. It's time to call out every self-sabotaging thought or feeling you have. If you really want to reduce your stress and feel more fulfilled in life, you have to look these lovingly in the face. Not in a judgemental way. In an 'I'm your best friend, and I want to support you in life' way. So, let's be really honest; lovingly and encouragingly. Get them all out of your closet, and get them onto paper. How exactly are you being your own worst enemy? You have to own all your thoughts and feelings; otherwise they will continue to get in your way.

What are your self-judgements? How about your self-doubt? What are your very own 'I'm not good enough' beliefs? How about your 'I could never do/be/have that' beliefs? Even the 'there's no point because' beliefs. Let's see them. All of them.

Now, look at that list. What would your best friend say about those things? I know that all those judgements and beliefs are a part of who you are right now but you can free yourself from any of these – if you want to.

Yes, it is going to take some effort, and it would be easier not to bother at all. But if you don't bother, you won't change. And that's why you're reading this book, isn't it? Because you want to change. You want to be happier and more fulfilled. You don't want to be stressed or anxious.

So, to look at this list through the loving eyes of your own-best-friend-self: look at each thing you have written down and know that at some point in your life, it served a purpose, so make peace with it.

Then go through your entire list, one thing at a time, and ask yourself:

- Do I still need that judgement or belief now?
- Does it serve me? If so, how?
- Or, do I want to let that go now?

Write your answers down. Don't just skip through it in your head. I say that because I can be the world's worst at understanding the theory but not doing the required practice to *actually* make a real difference (the irony that I have just made a comment about me being the world's worst in the #hack about being your own-worst-enemy-self!).

Writing things down gets you to look at them – and own them – at a deeper level. It's transformational. When you have looked at them in this way you are more likely to spot them when they are playing out in your everyday life. You will have more chance of interrupting those self-sabotaging own-worst-enemy-self reactions and replacing them with own-best-friend-self responses.

More about becoming your own-best-friend-self in the next #hack, but please don't skip this bit first. Your own-worst-enemy-self would definitely try to skip this.

## # The hack

Through the lens of your loving and supportive own-best-friend-self, take the time and effort to write down all the ways that you are your own-worst-enemy-self. Make peace with them. Review which ones you still want to keep, and which ones you are ready to let go of. Let any emotion that surfaces be there – it's all part of releasing that which no longer serves you.

Look out for moments where your own-worst-enemy-self is surfacing in everyday life. Use the single-breath practice (#hack 3) to interrupt it and consider what a more supportive response would be in that moment.

# BECOMING YOUR OWN-BEST-FRIEND-SELF

If we were to write a list of the qualities that an ideal best friend would have, it would likely include things like: being supportive, honest, kind, fun, a good listener, genuine, trustworthy, encouraging, loving and always there for us when we need them.

How lovely. And we are very lucky if we have someone like that in our lives, so a shout out to them. We are likely that person for another, or others, so a shout out to you too.

The question is: why aren't we being that for ourselves? And, what would life be like if we were?

You see, being all those things to yourself really has nothing to do with whether anyone else is being those things for you. Nobody gets in the way of you loving and supporting yourself, except you. And that can change. I hope it does.

You already are supportive, honest, kind, trustworthy and loving. You just need to be that to yourself, as well as to others.

So, what would it look like if you were to be your own-best-friend-self? Well, firstly, every time your own-worst-enemy-self showed up, you would reassure it, and say 'it's OK, we've got this'. Your own-best-friend-self would be right by your side every time you find yourself outside of your comfort zone. In those moments of self-doubt, your own-best-friend-self will tell you you're amazing and that you can do this.

When you are upset, in any way at all, your own-best-friend-self will listen to you in a supportive and totally non-judgemental way. It will say: 'I hear you'.

When you are struggling or stressed, they will ask you: 'What do you need? Is there anything I can do?'

When you are on your knees, or when the tears are rolling down your face, your own-best-friend-self will get a box of tissues and sit with you, without trying to hurry you out of what you are feeling.

When you have totally messed up, your own-best-friend-self won't judge you. Rather, they will encourage you that you can do better next time.

When you are behaving like a total idiot or being stroppy, your own-best-friend-self will call you out, non-judgementally and supportively. They will mediate between where you are and what you aren't seeing.

When you get too blinkered and can't see the wood for the trees, they will help you see what you cannot.

When you're bored, stuck or need uplifting, your own-best-friend-self will say: 'Come on, let's go do this'.

Your own-best-friend-self will be there to support you in every way they can. They won't judge you, or your mistakes. But they will hold you accountable to be the amazing person they know you to be. They won't have you thinking small about yourself, because that's not who you are. They see the best in you, and it's that that they support you to be.

You can be all of that, for you. And why on earth wouldn't you be all of that? Why wouldn't you be the love that you are, to yourself?

It's time for you to go all in. Life really is too short not to.

You need to decide if you are prepared to make a full commitment to supporting, encouraging and loving yourself – just like a true friend would. I mean that. I want with all my heart for you to stop being your own-worst-enemy-self and start giving yourself the love and support that you deserve. Sure, other people might also do that. They might not. But you can, and you have no doubt wasted enough of your life not doing so. Can you imagine how much easier life would be if you actually started to help yourself? If you looked after yourself? If you gave yourself a chance and a bit of encouragement?

This is where being present will come in again. You need to catch yourself in the act when you're being your own-worst-enemy-self. You need to interrupt that habit and, at that moment, ask yourself: 'What would my own-best-friend-self do or say right now?' Then you need to act on that.

It will take time to change the habit, but you can if you want to. I can't do this for you. I am here encouraging you, just like your best friend would, but you need to make the choice. Will you start supporting yourself, or won't you? Will you start respecting yourself, or won't you? Will you start loving yourself, or won't you? Will you give yourself a chance, or won't you?

# The hack

It's time to start being your very own-best-friend-self. To start supporting and encouraging yourself in life. Every time your own-worst-enemy-self makes an appearance, use the single-breath practice (#hack 3) to pause enough to ask yourself: 'What would my own-best-friend-self say and do now?'

Your own-best-friend-self will always have your best interests at heart, and will hold you accountable to be the amazing person that you are.

# R.E.S.P.E.C.T.

If you are a bit of a people-pleaser and/or you avoid conflict, you might find that, at times, you lack a bit of self-respect. Not intentionally, but because you are so busy keeping everyone else happy and bending over backwards not to offend them, you often trample all over yourself. You put up with things that you wouldn't expect anyone else to. You make excuses for people and the way that they treat you.

Your own-best-friend-self wouldn't do that. They would tell you to politely tell some people where to stick it. I'm not suggesting that you do but I am suggesting that you check in with your level of self-respect. What do you allow that you later resent?

You see, without realizing it, when we do this we sign up to play our very own victim role. We go along with things that we feel are disrespectful, we say nothing, and then we feel disrespected. The irony is we haven't noticed that it is us disrespecting ourselves for allowing it. We set the tone. We set the standards for others to follow.

You might want your own-best-friend-self to check in with the people and the situations in your life that you feel disrespected in. Notice the part you are playing in allowing that. Where are you treating yourself with a lack of respect? Are there conversations you need to have? Are there any boundaries that need adjusting?

If you are loving to yourself, you won't treat yourself with a lack of respect and you won't let other people do it either. Once you have self-respect, you will find that people tend to treat you with it too. You will find one of the side-effects of self-respect is a significant drop in stress levels, along with a considerable rise in self-confidence and inner peace. Who would have thought!

Time to respect the amazing person you are, don't you think?! I know it might not be quite as easy as that, so if you need help doing it, read #hack 33 on a daily basis.

## # The hack

Recognize when you are trampling all over yourself and putting up with things that you don't like. Know that it is you that is going along with that, so it is you that needs to put a stop to it. If you need help with this, refer to #hack 33 for a daily reminder.

Breathe. Stand tall. You've got this!

# PERFECTLY PERFECT

Another own-worst-enemy-self tactic that causes a great deal of stress is perfectionism. People stress themselves out by thinking they should automatically, and always, be brilliant at everything they do. They compare everything they do with an illusionary ideal; one which, of course, they never reach. It's totally nuts if we think about it, so let's unpick this craziness a bit more.

If you get a new job, for example, you'd expect it to take time to become familiar with what's required and how things are done – and yet you expect yourself to hit the floor running as if you've been there forever.

If you had just newly qualified at something, you would expect it to take time before you had the wealth of experience that an expert would have, and yet you expect it of yourself immediately. That hobby you start – well, you are criticizing how useless you are before you have even given it, or you, a chance. Your hair – well, that's mostly a disaster isn't it? You're never quite thin or fit enough either, are you? You are not committed enough to your job, or your family, and you are a terrible friend.

I could go on... but, wowsers! It's exhausting, isn't it? And yet, we do it.

I have even had to give myself a talking to writing this book. I can't tell you how many times I have procrastinated about doing it because I wanted to make sure I was going to write the best possible book I could. On the day I agreed to get the draft to the publisher, I had a total wave of Imposter Syndrome, and of feeling like a total idiot for thinking I could write a book in the first place. I am sure that had my own-best-friend-self not seen this coming and made sure I had already committed to it, then my own-worst-enemy-self would have backed out, or delayed again.

Perfectionism is a mindset that guarantees self-induced stress. When people tell me that a lot of their stress is 'just because they are perfectionists', they often say it as if that's a good thing. Like it's a badge of honour that says 'I have high standards'. I can tell you that having high standards is nothing to do with perfectionism. Perfectionism is harsh self-judgement and a lack of self-love and self-worth. It stops us from getting started with the things we really want to do. It gets in the way of us being the brilliant selves that we already are, and all that we will become.

If you are a perfectionist, give yourself permission to be a student in life because the irony is that if you allow yourself to do this, you will far exceed all that you are achieving and being now. Give yourself permission to do your best and enjoy the fact that your future best may well be better than your current one. That's the point. That's what we are all here for. We can do our best and we can keep learning. Your own-best-friend-self would tell you that and encourage you to have a go at things. Keep your high standards, but recognize that they are nothing to do with perfectionism.

If you have made a commitment to become your own-best-friend-self, and I truly hope that you have, then you will lovingly start to be a bit more patient and forgiving with yourself. If you truly want to achieve the best you can, then you will accept that doing your best is enough.

Next time you find yourself trying that new hobby, let yourself be a beginner. When you are doing a project at work that means a lot to you, give yourself permission to do what you can, with what you have and where you are.

Do your best *and* love yourself along the way. It doesn't have to be an either/or. And like me, let your own-best-friend-self give you a good talking to every time you are slipping into those perfectionism tendencies.

## # The hack

Recognize that perfectionism has nothing to do with having high standards. Perfectionism is an own-worst-enemy-self tactic showing up as harsh self-judgement and a lack of self-love and self-worth.

Allow yourself to be a student in life, and get your own-best-friend-self to give you a good talking to every time perfectionism tries to self-sabotage what you are doing.

# Part 6

# SELF-CARE

Do you look after yourself? Does your lifestyle support the life you want to lead?

Mmmmmm. I suspect that, in the grand scheme of things, and in all that you have to do, you often put yourself at the bottom of the to-do list. I suspect that self-care isn't one of your priorities right now, if it ever has been.

I don't know about you but, every now and then, I recognize that I have slipped into habits that aren't in alignment with who I want to be. Sometimes I know that they aren't supporting me as well as they could, especially when feeling stressed. The thing about habits is that they quickly become unconscious choices – which is a good thing if the habit is a supportive one. It's not great when it isn't.

That needs to change.

Part 6 is going to help you to get back on track with self-care. It's going to help you to find the supportive habits you need to thrive in life. In short, we're about to kick your lifestyle into touch to make sure you are getting all the love and care you deserve.

From this moment on, you are going to value yourself enough to realize that you need looking after. You can't do all that you want to do if you don't look after yourself. Deep down, you know that. You just haven't taken the time to look after yourself.

That's going to change. From now on, every single day, say to yourself these four essential words:

## *I'm worth caring for.*

# GIVE YOURSELF A BREAK

When was the last time you relaxed? I mean, really relaxed.

The literal definition of relaxed is being free from tension and anxiety, which is a rare experience for many people. The first time I tried a restorative yoga class, it was entirely removed from my preferred active style of yoga practice. I was a doing sort of a person, rather than a being type. Restorative yoga is about stillness, nurturing and, as the name suggests, restoring. It invites you to let go of effort and tension. It's being rather than doing.

The experience proved insightful to say the least. I had no idea just how much stress I held in my body until I gave it time to let go of it all. I mean, it wasn't like I felt tense in everyday life, and I certainly wasn't aware of tension in my body. I wasn't aware of the tension I held in my mind or emotions either, but they were there all the same. In restorative yoga, all postures are floor-based, so either seated or lying down. They are entirely supported, so there is no muscular effort at all.

*No effort at all.* How often are you like that, other than when sleeping?

Initially, it took a while for me to settle into doing nothing. It took time for my mind and body to let go of things they didn't even know they were holding. The most humbling observation was that, having started to do so, my body, mind and emotions continued to let go throughout the entire practice.

I was amazed that even when I thought my body was relaxed and didn't have any more tension to release, as the minutes went by, it continued to find more and more ease. The practice took me to places of ease that made me realize just how much tension I carried in everyday life. I know I am not alone, and many people can relate to the same lack of ease.

Finding this state of ease is so important for our health and wellbeing on every level. Our hyper-productivity is literally depriving our nervous system of optimal functioning. I have already talked quite a lot about the role that relaxation plays in switching off the fight-or-flight response in our nervous system. Making time to relax is often the first thing that disappears when we are super busy. But it shouldn't be. Doing something that we find relaxing helps to balance out the high intensity of pressure that is part of leading a successful and busy life.

In the super-busy life you might be leading, do you ever allow yourself a lazy day? Do you ever give yourself permission to do nothing productive at all? Aside from offering us some much-needed rest and time to unplug, doing nothing can be the most productive thing we could do. Even being bored has benefits. From boredom, inspiration can arise. Giving yourself permission to totally blob out for a day can feel utterly decadent.

I am not suggesting that you do it full-time. I am suggesting you do it every now and then. If the very thought of doing this freaks you out, then you probably need it more than anyone. If you are going to start looking after yourself, you not only need to find the time and the way to relax; you also need to give yourself permission to do so.

We all find different things relaxing, so it's about finding something that works for you. I find that state of total relaxation comes through my regular practice of meditation. I use breath awareness to weave it into my everyday life. I find sitting having a cup of tea and watching the birds in my garden relaxing, and it's often a daily occurrence. Walking around the nature reserve in the village is something I do several times a week. I love having a massage but only have one every now and then (note to self: book one in).

What do you find relaxing? What is something you do daily to relax? What do you do periodically, if not daily? What would you like to do more often than you currently do?

## Enjoyment and fun

The same goes for enjoyment, which can also be relaxing but it might not be. I love skiing and playing golf but I wouldn't always say they are relaxing. Doing things that we enjoy helps us to handle our challenges in life. It gives us a more positive outlook in life, especially when we work hard or have something going on that could be completely consuming. Rather like relaxation, there can be things we enjoy daily, frequently and less frequently. Having stuff in the diary to look forward to can keep us motivated and inspired in life.

This is where being present comes in again. Being fully present in these moments makes life feel more fulfilling. Your own-best-friend-self would tell you to leave your phone alone and really allow yourself to relax and enjoy the moment. To embrace the whole felt experience of it all. Being present in the things we enjoy celebrates the fact that life is precious.

Don't put life off for *when you've got time*. Let go of doing things that you no longer enjoy. Let the friendships that you have grown out of drift away. Let yourself grow into things that bring you joy now. Go to places that you enjoy going to. In the busy world that we find ourselves in, it can be good to remind ourselves of some very wise words that Gandhi said: 'There is more to life than just increasing its speed'.

# # The hack

Give yourself permission to make time to relax. Recognize that it plays an essential part in you functioning at the high level that you want to. The same goes for enjoyment and fun. They make life fulfilling, help us to feel truly alive and fire us up to better handle any challenges we face.

# BORN TO MOVE

Our bodies are designed to move. We know that exercise has the potential to positively influence our mental, emotional and physical wellbeing. It has been proven to help manage the symptoms of stress and boost our energy levels. The question is: what exercise supports you?

At different stages of life, how we exercise is likely to change. What we used to be able to do, or have time to do, might change. I used to love going to the gym. Now I would rather be outside walking or doing yoga. It's changed, as it might for you. The main thing is to find something that works for you in your current life.

Our all-or-nothing mentality can get in the way of regular exercise. If you like running marathons, for example, and you find yourself working long hours and/or with a family, it would be easy to quit running altogether because you haven't got time to run a marathon. Trying to find time to run even for half an hour twice a week might feel pointless because you are not aiming for a race, but it would be better than not running at all. I know there are guidelines as to how much and how often we should be exercising but my own personal advice is that anything is better than nothing.

If you currently don't do any exercise at all, maybe it's time for your own-best-friend-self to encourage you to

145

commit to even just one exercise session a week. There are so many online exercise classes now that you needn't even leave the house – ideal if you have kids or can't afford to join a class. Bring in other incremental steps like taking the stairs rather than the lift. Go for a walk at lunchtime. Go out for a walk or a bike ride with friends or family at the weekend. Whatever works for you as the best way to let exercise into your life will be worth it.

I should also say that while exercise is mostly good for us, it can be used in a harmful way too. Excessive exercise can be a coping strategy that ends up being self-abusive. So while the majority of people need encouragement to fit more exercise into their lives, some need loving support to reduce it. Like any other addiction, if training is getting in the way of living a healthy, functional life, then it is time to seek advice and address what's behind it.

Exercise, when done in a nurturing way, will reduce your stress and give you the energy and inspiration that you seek. It will help you to sleep and will help you to relax. It will enable you to be the brilliant person that you are.

## # The hack

If you want more energy, better-quality sleep and less stress, you need to exercise. You need to exercise in a way that supports and nurtures the successful life you want to lead, and the physical capabilities that you have.

Does your relationship with exercise help you? What incremental step in the right direction could you commit to now? Remember, anything is better than nothing.

# POSTURE POWER

While on the subject of exercise, it seems fitting (no pun intended) to touch upon posture now too. We all have one, but whether it's helping us or not is another matter. Posture can either help keep our body problem-free, or it can contribute to causing problems.

Stress can have an enormous effect on our posture. Think of the typical posture of a depressed person, for example: they might have rounded shoulders with their head and gaze lowered towards the floor. A shy person tends to make themselves smaller. An irate person might puff themselves up. An anxious person might have visibly raised shoulders and tension across their face.

Then there is the posture we end up in from what we spend most of our time doing. For example, a slumped posture with the head projected forward can be typical of anyone that spends many hours at a computer, and can lead to the kyphotic spine that some elderly people end up with. Long term, this posture causes strain on the musculature system and a restrictive breath pattern.

Checking your posture regularly at random points throughout the day can save you from developing all sorts of problems. Try noticing it when you are driving, walking, sitting at a desk, eating lunch or having a conversation. I used to have a poor driving posture before I got into yoga. I was very much a laid-back, one hand on the wheel kind of driver. Once I got into yoga, I noticed that I became more comfortable sitting up straighter. I adjusted my seat into a more upright position, which put far less stress on my neck. Another benefit of improving my posture was that long-haul travel in economy became far more comfortable (OK, so I would love to travel first class, but in the meantime…) and the adverse effects of travel were massively reduced.

Talking of driving, if you happen to be someone who checks yourself out in the rear-view mirror fairly regularly, you might sit slightly leaning over to the left. Next time you get into the driver's seat, sit up straight in your seat with both feet on the floor. Without moving anything else, turn your head to look into your rear-view mirror. If the view out of the rear windscreen is not centred, you probably sit leaning over to the left as a result of frequently checking yourself out! It might seem insignificant, but over time habits create posture and sometimes create problems, and this particular position can lead to scoliosis, as can carrying young children on one hip, or heavy bags in one hand only.

It's not just about the physical problems that posture can cause though. In the same way that our mood can affect our posture, so too can our posture influence our mood.

Social psychologist Amy Cuddy's 2012 TED talk 'Your body language may shape who you are' has had over 16 million views and highlights the relationship between mind and body.[10] In her talk, Amy shares the result of an experiment studying the effects of positive posture

---

[10] A. Cuddy, *Your body language may shape who you are*, 2012. Available from www.ted.com/talks/amy_cuddy_your_body_language_may_shape_who_you_are?language=en [accessed 28 January 2020].

(superwoman pose, or the alpha male one of hands on head, elbows out wide) and negative posture (dropped shoulders, head down, folded arms) on testosterone and cortisol. The study group were split into two groups: one adopting positive posture and the other negative posture, both for a few minutes each. During this time, testosterone (dominance hormone) and cortisol (response to stress) levels were monitored.

The study found that adopting a positive posture resulted in a rise in testosterone and a drop in cortisol, with the opposite result in negative posture. What does this mean? Well, our physiological response to posture affects the way we feel. A rise in testosterone helps us to feel more confident and in control, while an increase in cortisol is a sign that we feel under threat.

If you think about this in the context of time, given that these results happened in just a few minutes, can you imagine the ongoing effects of posture all day, every day? While only a small study, it does highlight the relationship between mind and body.

It's worth paying attention to your posture throughout the day, and whether changing your posture affects the way you feel. If you are feeling stressed or lacking in confidence and notice you are walking around with rounded shoulders and your head down, maybe it's worth standing up taller, rolling your shoulders back and lifting your gaze to see if it elevates your mood and confidence levels. Surely it's worth a try!

We read each other's body language without giving it any thought. When someone walks into the room in a slumped posture, with their gaze lowered towards the floor, it doesn't take rocket science to observe that they might not be having a great day. Likewise, if someone is rushing about, out of breath, with visibly tense shoulders, it's obvious they are not relaxed.

While our body language tells a story to others, it also affects the way the world responds to us. A neutral, open posture is approachable and accessible to others. You will have a more expanded view of the world around you. Posture is a free tool that can serve you well, so it is worth being mindful of the message you are giving to the world around you, and the message you are giving to yourself.

## # The hack

Check your posture regularly at random points throughout the day. Try noticing it when you are driving, walking, sitting at a desk, eating lunch or having a conversation. Is it helping you or hindering you? What message is it giving to the world around you?

# BODY LOVE

Do you love and respect the body you have? Do you love and accept your uniqueness, exactly as you are?

Poor self-image seems to be on the rise and the pressure to look a certain way can be immensely overwhelming for some. Lack of love for the body is really a lack of love for the self.

It saddens me to see the current trend of cosmetic surgery with many people never feeling satisfied with how they look. I have been there myself when I had my breasts enlarged in my early thirties. I had just left my first husband, and I desperately wanted to find love. Looking back, I only had them done because I thought that's what men liked and I thought mine weren't big enough. I believed that having them would make me more attractive and more likely to find love.

Of course, I realized in hindsight that it wasn't the answer. I know people talk a lot about finding self-acceptance and at the time I had my breasts enlarged I didn't see that as a big deal, when clearly it was. Having larger breasts felt like it gave me more confidence and self-acceptance. They certainly got me more attention – but it was as fake as they were, and eventually I realized that. When one of them ruptured, ironically just after my second husband left me,

I had them both removed. I feel self-love and acceptance now, and the scars remind me of my journey to it.

Happiness really does come from accepting, loving and respecting the body we have been given. When you care for yourself, you want to look after your body. Diet and exercise choices come from a desire to nurture instead of self-criticism (see #hack 40). There will always be somebody younger, better looking, fitter or whatever else we might think we need to be more like.

When we embrace being the unique individual that we are, insecurities start to drop away – as does the stress that goes with it. I am not telling anyone that they should or shouldn't have cosmetic surgery – but just to recognize that in and of itself it is unlikely to fix their lack of self-love and self-worth. I get that part of being human is having a physical attraction to particular looks or types, but underneath all of that we are all looking for love and a deeper connection – whatever package that comes in.

## Sensational

We don't just benefit from noticing when our body is trying to tell us when something is wrong or what it needs. Being in tune with our body can also increase the richness of life's experiences of all the amazing sensations our body can have. Have you noticed how good having a shower can feel, or a soak in a hot bath? Are you able to feel a cool breeze on your skin or the warmth of the sun? How great it feels to sit down after being on your feet all day? Or to move, having sat down all day? In moments of intimacy, are you fully present and noticing how your body responds to touch? Do you know which fabrics your skin loves you to wear, and which it prefers you not to? Getting in touch with what your body is trying to tell you can only bring greater health and joy. Don't we all want that?

# The hack

Seriously… quit the self-criticism. Your body is amazing. Love your body and love yourself. You are absolutely enough!

Start noticing the joy of sensation. Your body is alive.

# FUEL YOUR BRILLIANCE

We are what we eat. Well, not literally, but our wellbeing certainly depends on what we eat. Different cultures have different ideas about exactly what a healthy diet looks like but they probably all hint towards eating fresh, whole foods. I am not a nutritionist, but I can share with you a few useful tips on how to create a healthier relationship with food.

If you are being your own-best-friend-self, you will want to look after yourself. You won't be basing your food choices on looking a certain way. You will be basing them on making sure you have the ability to live a vibrant life. You will want to eat the food that will give you all the nutrients you need, and you will want to enjoy eating it. Your own-best-friend-self won't advise you to crash diet. Ever. Your own-best-friend-self will encourage you to ditch eating rubbish – the least-processed food, the better. It will interrupt your emotional eating by asking you what's wrong and giving you a hug before you reach for the biscuits.

The topic of what to eat could be a book in and of itself. I recommend seeing a nutritionist if you don't know where to start and want more personal guidance.

In the meantime, these five suggestions can get you started in fuelling your brilliance…

# Mindful food choices

Before you choose anything, ask yourself: 'Will this choice nourish me or drain me?' If you are a comfort eater, ask yourself: 'Am I eating this because of how I am feeling?' If that's a yes, ask yourself what else you could do instead? Could you take a few conscious breaths and acknowledge how you feel? Go for a quick walk? Get a drink of water? As your own-best-friend-self looking after your wellbeing, you will suggest to yourself that eating that cake halfway through the morning might feel like a good idea but it will only make your energy levels crash later. Sugar plays havoc with our blood sugar levels and mood swings, so it is rarely in our best interests.

# Mindful eating

Have you ever eaten a whole bar of chocolate without even noticing? Or drank a glass of wine without tasting any of it after the first sip? Have you eaten an entire plate full of dinner while watching TV? Yes, me too. We would enjoy our food far more, and easily self-regulate, if we were fully present when eating. So if you really want to enjoy what you eat, then notice what you eat. It's life-changing! Bring your awareness into the taste and texture of your food. Don't eat while you are scrolling through emails, social media or work.

# Plan ahead

Diet choices can often be time related. It really will pay dividends if you plan some healthy meals in advance. You can make batches of healthy meals to freeze so that they can become your fast food. Take healthy snacks to work. Even if you only replace one bar of chocolate or one biscuit snack with an apple and some nuts, it's a start.

## Drink more water

If you are a fizzy drink addict, then try replacing half the amount you are currently drinking with water.

Reduce your caffeine and alcohol intake. Neither of them are your friends if you suffer from anxiety, stress, depression or other mental health issues as among many other effects, they both interfere with sleep quality. Too much caffeine can make even the most level-headed person feel jittery and anxious. When one of my clients said she was feeling completely overwhelmed with life and highly anxious, I suggested she cut out caffeine. She was amazed at just how much of her anxiety disappeared from that one choice alone. However many cups of caffeinated tea or coffee you have a day – start reducing it, replacing it with herbal tea or hot water and fresh lemon.

Have at least three alcohol-free nights a week. If you drink wine, then try drinking a wine spritzer with fizzy water rather than straight wine. Small incremental steps are life-changing. Reduction is better than doing nothing at all. If you feel you would benefit from cutting either caffeine or alcohol out completely, then do it.

## Try an 80/20 approach

By this I mean: eat healthily 80% of the time and allow yourself 20% for human nature! OK, so some of you won't eat into the 20%. Healthy eating is about getting into habits that support and nourish you.

Despite the often conflicting dietary advice that seems to be out there, there are a few fundamentals that aren't rocket science. We know that eating a diet high in sugar and carbs increases our chances of inflammatory conditions, diabetes and obesity. We know that eating more calories than we are using will result in weight gain, and eating fewer calories than we are using will result in weight loss. We know that we need a variety of nutrients from fresh whole foods to nourish us and keep us in tip-top form. Most of us would find the 80/20 approach far more sustainable than an all-or-nothing approach.

## # The hack

Love yourself enough to want to look after your wellbeing, and to make dietary choices that nourish and support you. Assuming that you want to feel healthy and vibrant, what incremental dietary changes can you fully commit to that will better support you and the life you wish to lead? Don't put this off. Start today.

# ZZZZZZZZZ'S

How much sleep do you get each night?

Until I did further research into sleep earlier this year, I hadn't quite appreciated just what a key part of our entire wellbeing it is. To be honest with you, I used to believe that as we are all individuals, how much sleep we needed would vary. I tended to take the recommended seven to nine hours with a pinch of salt because so many people do get varied amounts of sleep and seem to be surviving.

As it turns out, the recommendation of having seven to nine hours' sleep a night is pretty well-founded. Not one part of our mental, emotional or physical functioning isn't affected by sleep. Some processes occur during sleep that take a good seven to nine hours to effectively complete. If we cut those short, we deprive ourselves of the benefits. I highly recommend reading *Why We Sleep* by Professor Matthew Walker.[11] It will give you all the info you need on how to get a good night's sleep and why we should. Seemingly, 'not needing' much sleep isn't at all cool. Sleep, and plenty of it, is the new sexy and super-cool.

For the benefit of giving you a better night's sleep and significantly reducing your stress, here are a few tips:

---

[11] M. Walker, *Why we sleep: The new science of sleep and dreams*, 2018.

- Keep your bedroom a cool, clean and tidy sanctuary. Ideally around 18 degrees Celsius. Use blackout blinds if there is too much light outside. Keep the room clutter-free.
- *Leave your phone and all other screens out of the bedroom.* Yep, that needs to be emphasized. If you use your phone for an alarm – get an alarm clock.
- Try to keep a regular sleep schedule. Try to go to bed at the same time each night, give or take half an hour. Get up at the same time every day – even if you have gone to bed extra-late the night before. Don't use a snooze button. Get out of bed as soon as your alarm goes off.
- Do a breath-awareness practice for ten minutes before you go to bed, and at any point that you wake up in the night and can't sleep. The diaphragmatic breath practice in #hack 4 would be a good one, as would keeping the exhalation slightly longer than the inhalation.
- Get outside for a minimum of 30 minutes every day, ideally in the morning.
- Cut out caffeine from 12pm onwards (assuming you follow a normal awake in the day/sleep at night pattern rather than work night shifts). Cut out all caffeine if you have sleep issues.
- Cut down on alcohol or completely cut it out.
- Address any issues that are keeping you awake at night (see #hack 11). We sleep better when we are actively taking part in resolving any problems we are facing.

There are so many things we can do to get a good night's sleep, so it's worth giving these suggestions a try if you're not getting seven to nine hours. All that said, don't stress yourself out if you aren't getting enough sleep. There are times in life when we just won't. At these times, more than ever, use the breathing techniques to help switch on the rest and digest part of the nervous system. It is one thing lying in bed at night awake and relaxed, and another thing lying in bed at night wired and stressed. The breath practices can make that difference.

# # The hack

Get seven to nine hours' sleep a night to significantly reduce your stress levels, and make your life a whole lot easier. If you don't get this amount on a regular basis then try any of the suggestions in this #hack. I highly recommend reading *Why We Sleep* by Professor Matthew Walker.

# MONEY, MONEY, MONEY

Talking of a good night's sleep, something that can definitely get in the way of it is money. If you have ever struggled to pay your bills, you will know how stressful that is. In a world where we are bombarded with all the things we could have/do/be and where many things can be financed, it's worth reviewing what's worth financing and what isn't. We all have different views on these things. Beyond having a roof over our head and paying our bills, everything else seems to become relative. Living according to our means is one thing; living beyond our means another.

A few years ago, the subject of money came up in a stress management session I was doing with a group of factory workers. They were talking about the stress they felt at struggling to pay their monthly bills. They couldn't afford to go on holiday with their kids, and they were trying to work extra shifts to make ends meet. It's undoubtedly stressful to worry about not being able to afford a basic standard of living.

The day after this session, I was working with a group of solicitors, and they too were talking about being stressed about not being able to pay their bills each month. Though they earned a lot more than the factory workers, they had financed their lives up to the hilt to have the big house, the beautiful cars and the kids in private school. They were working extremely long hours to try to pay for it all. Undeniably, a completely different quality of living to the factory workers, but the same fear of not making ends meet each month. I highlight this because the lure of a better life isn't always a guarantee to get rid of feeling stressed – it can just move the goalposts.

What price would you pay for peace of mind? It's worth looking at your finances to see if what you are spending your money on is worth it. Does it serve a purpose and add value? Some debt is worth having. Some debt isn't. Consumerism thrives on you believing you are inadequate as you are, with what you have. It sells you the idea that if you buy that product, you will be more/better/someone else. Remember to find what feels right for you. Some decisions have longer-term consequences than others. Debt can be a heavy price to pay, so make sure it's worth it.

What I can share is that the more present you become in life, the more grateful you become and the less you *need* to make yourself happy. It seems to be a natural side-effect. I have found in my own life that, while I still like many beautiful things, I don't feel I need them. I am happy with them and happy without them. That, to me, is financial freedom. How about you?

# # The hack

Do a review of your finances and get financial advice if you want expert help. Make sure what you are spending your money on adds value to your life. Review your relationship with debt and financing your lifestyle. Is it a healthy one? For further reading, I recommend *The 6 Steps to Financial Freedom: How to Turn Your Debt into Wealth* by Immanuel Ezekiel.[12]

---

[12] I. Ezekiel, *The 6 steps to financial freedom: How to turn your debt into wealth*, 2011. See also Immanuel Ezekiel's website: www.the6stepstofinancialfreedom.com

# SYSTEM OVERHAUL

If you are trying to fit 50 hours of content into 24 hours, it won't work if you are trying to do it all yourself. It might work if you get help. When I look at a client's schedule with them to help make it more efficient, the first thing we do is look at all the areas that take time and effort but needn't do.

There are often simple solutions that make life much more doable. Things like getting a cleaner or a gardener – how many hours a week could that save? Sometimes people tell me they can't afford one but in most cases they can – it just means tweaking their finances to better use. How about getting groceries delivered rather than doing the shopping yourself? There's another hour saved for just a few quid. How about all members of the household helping out in the house? Teamwork.

If you have got too much to do in not enough time, go through a typical week and see what you could delegate. What else can you outsource in your life? Small shifts in these areas all add up to a successful working system.

As well as the practical support systems, how about the mental and emotional ones? Who are your go-to friends or family when you need moral support or an extra pair of hands? Who do you turn to for advice (see #hack 14)?

We are not on our own, and there are always people that can help. They need to be part of your support system. What about the rest of your team – your GP, hairdresser, massage therapist, personal trainer, neighbour, postman, accountant, kids' teachers, go-to electrician, plumber, local garage... You get the picture – get the whole team you need to be part of your slick operation. It all needs to support you.

Being successful in life requires a slick support system. Every medal-winning athlete needs a whole team behind them. They have systems in place at every level – physical, mental, logistical and financial. We are no different. See yourself as the athlete in your life and look at what you need to help you to succeed. Is it time you had a system upgrade? What adjustments could help your life run a little more smoothly?

## # The hack

Review your support systems. Do they support you to function optimally? What can you delegate around the home? What can you outsource to give yourself more time? Are your emotional and mental support systems in place? Who are your go-to people?

# Part 7

# THE INSIDE JOB

So far, much of this book has been about recognizing, owning and reorganizing all that isn't working in your life. It has focused on addressing the cause of your stress and learning to look after yourself in the process.

The breath has played a key part throughout. It's quite extraordinary how such a simple tool can positively affect so much. It literally gives you breathing space from all that you face, interrupting unconscious habitual patterns that no longer serve you and opening up enough of a gap to allow new possibilities to find you.

Accepting what's in your control, and what isn't, will certainly make your life less stressful. Hopefully, you have realized that much in the outer world isn't worth getting worked up about, and that it is a better use of your time and energy to focus on that which you can affect.

This final part is where real transformation begins.

What if you and your state of being had far more influence on your outer circumstances, and the world at large, than you realize?

What if you had the potential to find peace at the centre of any storm?

What if you could experience a level of joy and love that you have never experienced before?

## *Don't stop now…*

# SELF-MASTERY

Addressing the external causes of our stress will do much for our peace of mind and wellbeing. As will looking after, and respecting, ourselves as our own-best-friend-self would.

There will come a time though, if you haven't already got there, when you will realize that the only real way to alleviate stress is to address *you*. As Charles Swindoll wisely said: 'Life is 10% what happens to you and 90% how you react to it'. You, your internal state of being, along with all of your beliefs and mindsets, will not only determine the life you experience, but also the life that *you* create.

Whenever we face external challenges, it can be easy to get so fixated on them that we forget to start within. We might fail to notice that we have completely lost our centre, our common sense and our broader perspective. We may not have realized that we might be trying to solve the problem from the limited view of our fearful lens. Einstein knew that problems cannot be solved from that place when he famously said: 'Problems are never solved at the level of thinking that created them'.

Somehow, when faced with a challenge, we need to rise above any fear that we feel and find an elevated level of consciousness. But this can't happen if our internal state is chaotic. Learning to master our internal state is *the* most life-changing thing we can do. If you feel peaceful, generous and loving, you will respond to life in a peaceful, generous and loving way. If you feel fearful, limited and defensive, you will respond to life in a fearful, limited and defensive way.

In reality, we can't stop life happening, and it won't always go to plan, so learning to gain control over our internal state gives us the confidence that we will be able to handle whatever life brings our way. When we know that, we become less fearful of the future and can begin to relax into life.

That is why I have been harping on about the breath all the way through this book! It plays a vital role in settling an over-reactive nervous system, restoring rational thinking, calming nerves and helping us to feel safe. It is key to us being able to control our internal state. If you haven't quite taken this on board yet, then please do. I have worked with so many people whose lives have been totally transformed even by just using the single-breath practice, such is its potential power.

The practice of being more present in each moment will afford you the self-awareness to know what state of being you are responding to the moment from. Being your own-best-friend-self will also go a long way to ensuring you are in the best internal state that you can be.

So, perhaps the three most important things I have said so far in this book are:

1. Breathe
2. Get present
3. Be your own-best-friend-self

# Hack your limiting beliefs and mindsets

I love self-development. I love it because I know that it can bring freedom from limiting beliefs and mindsets. Self-development is amazing when it works alongside self-acceptance. We all have the potential to keep growing and moving beyond current limits. We also all have the potential to love ourselves along the way. That, I believe, is where the real alchemy takes place. When self-development comes from a place of love, we already know that we are enough and that we can continue to expand and evolve with life itself.

When I go into organizations to run sessions on managing stress, and I talk about our true nature being kind, loving, generous and collaborative, a silence and a stillness fills the entire room. It does so because people know that I am right. They know that I am describing them, exactly as they are. As I do so, it almost moves them to tears at the realization they have lost themselves in their stress. I do not speak to people's stresses. I speak to them. To who they really are. To the brilliance that I know them to be.

I am doing the same to you now. I know you are not your stresses. You are not your limiting beliefs or mindsets either. You are more than that. We all are.

It is for this reason that I feel so passionate about helping you to remove anything that gets in the way of you being your true nature. Your beliefs and your mindset will very likely be getting in your way. Mine get in my way too, and I constantly have to be on the lookout for them doing so.

If we were to strip all limiting beliefs and mindsets back to their very essence, they would all have two things in common. Fear and lack. Don't take my word for it though. If you go back to the list you made in #hack 32 when you called out your own-worst-enemy-self, you will see that they are all steeped in fear or lack. Every single item on your list is just a symptom of one or both of those two things. It is those two that sit at the root of all evils, so to speak.

At the broader, higher-consciousness, bigger-picture level, both of those problems are solved with a very simple and fail-proof answer: love. Not just any old human love; it's more than that. For now though, and what's just as necessary, is the more practical, day-to-day approach of dealing with fear and lack showing up in our limiting beliefs and mindsets.

So, while fear and lack underpin all negative thoughts and feelings, we all need to find our own practical approach to how we move beyond them. This is one of those areas where there really isn't a one-size-fits-all approach. Whatever limiting belief or fear is holding you back, there is an answer to it. There will be an approach that works for you. You just need to find what resonates with you.

Let's use the belief that 'I am not enough' as an example. This will show up in all sorts of ways for different people. It might show up by not putting yourself forward for a promotion because 'you don't feel good enough to, and you're not experienced enough or knowledgeable enough'. It might show itself by you self-sabotaging your relationships because you are convinced that your partner will run off with someone 'better than you'. There are many ways it can show up, and the most effective way to approach overcoming it is to start by working with something that is specific to you. The thing that's most obvious to you.

When you have identified that, Google is a great place to start. Type in any issue and you will get an abundance of free information to help you. Perhaps there is a book or a podcast you come across, and that helps you. You might find a workshop or course that you could go to. Maybe you come across a specific coach or professional you want to work with. Whatever help you need, it's out there.

What I am saying is: do something. Own that you want to move beyond the belief that holds you back, and find the right approach for you in tackling it. Be focused on your strategy though or you won't actually action anything.

Let's say you lack confidence. Firstly, identify how you lack confidence. Is it in all areas or a specific one? If it's in all areas, which area affects you the most? Pick one particular area to focus on. So, let's go with someone lacking confidence in speaking to new people. Google that. Watch some YouTube videos on it. Listen to podcasts on it. Read a book if you come across one that sounds interesting to you. Then from all of that, write down a plan of action in how you will start applying what you are learning to your own life. Small steps, but determined goals that you intend to achieve. Then keep going.

Reflect on the progress you are making. If it's all working and you are happy that it's no longer holding you back (even if meeting new people will never be your favourite thing), then you're all good. If you're still stuck, then Google confidence coaches and see if there is a local one you can work with; or an online coach or course. And, just when you might think about giving up, remember that your own-best-friend-self would tell you not to. They would say to you to keep looking and that you are already making progress. Which you are. Keep encouraging yourself to move forward, taking one next step at a time. Even though it takes effort. Keep your eye on the prize, which is you, as your future free-from-this-issue-self. Don't believe it? Well, your own-best-friend-self will believe it for you, so keep going.

The truth is that you can master anything you put your mind to. You have to decide to help yourself. You have to decide that you want to overcome anything that holds you back from being the amazing person you can be. As Yoda, in all of his wisdom, wisely said: 'We are what we grow beyond'.

## # The hack

Own your internal state of being. Choose for it to be 100% your priority no matter what you face in life. Breathe.

Make a commitment to yourself to grow beyond your limiting beliefs and mindsets. They are not who you are.

# HACK INTO INNER PEACE

If you have applied what you have so far read in this book, you should be experiencing less stress and more peace. Hopefully, you might also feel a bit more contentment and fulfilment. Even if you went no further than this, I would be surprised if the quality of your life hadn't improved and continued to do so.

But. There is way more to be felt. There is a deeper calling from your true nature that, until you fully connect to it, will still leave a subtle void. It is the reason that nothing else can provide lasting peace or fulfilment. Our external world can provide glimpses of the joy, peace and fulfilment that we crave, but only ever that – a glimpse. It comes and goes.

Whether it's finding who we think is *the one*, satisfaction through food, the love from a child, self-worth from a career, or security through having money; all offer the feeling we seek but can only ever be incomplete. If we rely on these to fulfil our needs, then should they leave us, we will plummet back into the empty void they once filled. We, in and of ourselves, will once again feel empty or incomplete on some level. We will still feel lacking. Lacking love. Lacking peace. Lacking joy.

If we seek lasting peace, we will eventually recognize that the outer world, along with everything and everyone in it, is not the answer. We will eventually find that the way to lasting peace is an inner journey, not an outer one. It is then that the real work begins and true peace can find us. I appreciate that all the way through this book I have said that we are all different and that no one size fits all, but the many different routes we take will all eventually lead us to this same crossroads. To the journey inwards.

## Meditation

I often say that meditation completely changed my life. It did. Meditation allowed me to experience a depth of unconditional peace and love that I had never felt before. Words do no justice in describing the felt experience of total oneness and love that arises for me in meditation. It is an overwhelming sense of coming home to everything that I am.

Not long after I started meditating in the late 1990s, I experienced the transcendental nature of it. I discovered that while meditating, I found myself to be in a state that transcended all pain, and all negative emotions and thoughts. It was astounding. I experienced a feeling of complete oneness and had no need for anything. Everything finally made sense. I sensed that the answers to all outer questions could be found by going within. It is why I have been meditating regularly ever since. I know that every time I feel lost or in pain, relief is found by going inward.

In the early days, I only experienced this state of being while actually in meditation, with a remnant of it lingering for a while after. Over the years, this state of being has become a more frequent occurrence that doesn't just happen when I am meditating. I am still far from it being my continual existence, but I find it easier and easier to connect with in everyday life.

I can only describe to you the way I feel and the experiences I have through meditation, all of which I will cover in this last part of the book. In doing so, you might recognize similar experiences if you have had them. If you have not, I hope that it sparks an interest for you in exploring the inner journey for yourself. As I have said, that inner journey of meditation has been life-changing for me. It sits within everything that I do, everything that I am and everything that I am yet to become.

## So, why else meditate?

Something quite amazing starts to happen to our awareness when we meditate. We begin to get insights that arise more and more frequently, and not just during meditation. We start to become infused with layers of information that had previously been hidden. Intuitive feelings and knowledge start to drop into our awareness, often out of the blue.

When I first started meditating, I also trained in alternative therapy, learning to tune into energy and work with crystals. As part of that training we had to do one-to-ones so I started to practise on friends, and then friends of friends. I started getting all sorts of intuitive insights into what was going on for them in life. When I began working with people that I had never met before, it was obvious that I had no way of knowing the information that I was getting. It became apparent to me that when we connect to a higher consciousness, which I had experienced through meditation, we are connected to collective energy and knowledge. Inspired thinking is a normal part of the higher consciousness that arises through practising meditation.

Over the years, I have learnt to follow the guidance that comes through to me in meditation. All of my workshops and courses have arisen through meditation. This book has come about because it came to me in meditation, as will the next two books that I have already had insight on. The answers to many problems arise through meditation, as does the immense peace that surrounds them.

I have often sat to meditate on specific problems that I am seeking answers to. If I sit with the intent of listening to any wisdom that can help, I usually find that it comes. Sometimes I get information that I know to be true, but my human egoic self doesn't want to hear it. Learning to differentiate between getting intuition from higher consciousness and the thoughts and desires that arise from the human egoic mind is all part of the process of meditating.

## Inner guidance

If we are too busy in life, and have not made time to turn inwards, we are unlikely to hear our own inner guidance. We are unlikely to hear it if we fill every spare moment with external stimulation, whether that's the phone, the radio, podcasts, music, TV, gaming or other people. These all seem harmless, and they are, other than when they completely block out any time or space to hear our own inner guidance. Some people do this intentionally because they are purposefully avoiding feeling or hearing what they would rather not. Assuming though that you aren't trying to avoid noticing your own inner guidance, how often do you allow yourself the time to listen to it?

Hearing your inner guidance can occur at any moment we choose to draw our focus away from external noise. The breath practices and mindfulness meditation allow this space, as might any other moment where you choose to be open to hearing it. While silence can help, you don't necessarily need to be in total silence. You could easily hear it when you are sitting listening to calming music. Potentially, but often only with practice, we can hear our inner guidance no matter what.

When I am talking about listening to inner guidance, I am not talking about listening to the constant mental chatter and feelings that most people are very aware of. I am talking about a deeper level of awareness and insight that comes from our true nature. I will also call this our higher self. It is the part of us that comes from love, not fear.

If you wish to hear this part of yourself, you will likely need to start a regular breath, mindfulness or meditation practice. It is not impossible to do it without these practices, but they can definitely help. I know that I used to be far too busy and driven to have heard this part of myself – that is, until I started the practice of meditation.

## Where do you start?

There are many different types of meditation and all have their place. My suggestion to you would be to try a variety of styles and work with one that resonates with you. Over the years, I have done many different meditations – guided visualizations, meditating with background music, mantra meditation, candle gazing, contemplative meditation, walking meditation and my favourite – simply sitting in silence with breath awareness. I also teach a variety of different styles because I know there are many routes of meditation that can all lead to the same destination.

You might like to find a local meditation group or centre which can give individual instruction. You can find thousands of practices online, and as I have already recommended, the Headspace app is a good place to start, as is my website, or simply typing 'meditation' into YouTube. There will definitely be one style that resonates with you more than others, so while it sounds a bit vague of me to suggest that you simply search online, I am a great believer in you being drawn to both the teacher and the style of meditation that is right for you personally.

Whatever you try, be patient with yourself. As you will have found with the breath or mindfulness practices, the mind can be incredibly busy – and that doesn't matter. If you stick with it, you will likely gain a level of peace and connection that you have been seeking your whole life. Life will change, as will you.

## # The hack

Have a go at meditation! Visit my website www. louiselloyd.life, try the Headspace mindfulness app,[13] search on YouTube or go to a local meditation centre. Stick with it. You don't even have to enjoy it or feel the point of it – you just need to do it. Try a variety of styles until you find one that works best for you. And don't expect to levitate instantly!

---

[13] For information on the Headspace app, see www.headspace.com

# YOU'RE SO MUCH MORE THAN YOU THINK

In his book, *The Power of Now*, Eckhart Tolle describes the night that changed his entire life.[14] Before that night, Eckhart had suffered from severe anxiety and depression, and had, on occasions, felt suicidal. On that evening, he thought to himself: 'I cannot live with myself any more'. It dawned on him that, in that statement, he had two selves. He questioned who the *I* was that could not live with the *self*.

He later fell asleep and when he woke up the next day, his entire life and the world that he lived in had changed. He realized that there were different levels to his consciousness, and that all of his suffering existed at the human egoic level of the self. But in addition he also existed at a higher level of consciousness where there was no pain and suffering.

Many philosophers, mystics and spiritual traditions all offer descriptions of these different aspects of self. They all point towards what I too have experienced – that while there is the part of me that exists in the human body (the Louise that is writing this book), there is also an aspect of

---

[14] E. Tolle, *The power of now*, 1999.

me that exists beyond, as well as within, the physical. I call that the higher self; Eckhart calls it consciousness.

When I speak of our true nature as being loving, kind and generous – it is the higher self that I am referring to. Our human self, or egoic self, while also part of who we are, is limited in its thinking. It is at this level that we experience lack, fear, pain and suffering.

The higher self does not, in my experience at least, experience any of those emotions or suffering. In my experience, the higher self exists only as peace, joy and love. I have found that it bears witness to human emotions, but in and of itself it doesn't feel them. It somehow transcends them all, without losing an all-encompassing, never-changing peace, joy and love.

That said, I have experienced a level that seems to go even beyond peace, joy and love. As I have previously said, my words do no justice at all in even attempting to describe it. They are at best clumsy, because the felt experience of higher consciousness is beyond words or thoughts. If you have ever experienced it, you will know what I mean. The many philosophers and mystics that have attempted to describe it do so far more eloquently than I could. Einstein points towards it on many occasions. Socrates, Rumi and Kahlil Gibran do so beautifully and poetically. I quite like the work of David R. Hawkins in his books *Letting Go* and *Transcending the Levels of Consciousness*.[15] Eckhart Tolle lives and teaches presence – I can't recommend reading his book, *The Power of Now*, highly enough.

---

[15] D. R. Hawkins, *Letting go: The pathway of surrender*, 2012; D. R. Hawkins, *Transcending the levels of consciousness*, 2006.

Once you have experienced awareness of your higher self, life really can't ever be the same again. I say that because once you are aware of the deep level of love and peace that is your true nature, you will realize that it can never leave you. You will have access to it alongside any human experience you go through. You will recognize that you are everything that you will ever need to be, and that you have everything you could ever want. This means it becomes impossible to feel fear or lack to the same level ever again, even though at a human level it is still possible to feel them.

You will realize that it is *you* that is creating your reality, and because of that you know that life is always happening for you, and because of you, never to you. It is the most empowering realization you will ever have. I don't feel it is within the context of this particular book to go too far into this subject, but the book would have been incomplete if I didn't share with you something that can transcend *all* of your stress – the fact that *you* transcend all of your stress.

Some of you will already be very familiar with what I am talking about. If you are, then I urge you to re-ignite your spiritual practice if it has in any way waned. If this concept is new to you, then I encourage you to perhaps start by allowing for the possibility that you are more than you think you are. You might want to read Eckhart's book, or any other that draws you towards a deeper spiritual enquiry.

# # The hack

Consider the possibility that you exist at a level of consciousness that transcends all of your stress, pain and suffering. Consider that you have access to that awareness at all times. You have access because it is who you really are. Re-ignite your spiritual practice if it has waned. Consider exploring a spiritual practice if this is new to you and if it sparks your interest.

# BEYOND DUALITY

Let me share with you how meditation can help us to overcome the duality of experiencing both pain and pleasure. Some of the suffering that can arise from pain, whether that's physical, mental or emotional, is our resistance to it being there. If you can let go of that resistance and learn to sit with it, you will find it easier to go through. I am not suggesting that by doing that, we ignore it or don't address its cause. What I am suggesting is that if you *are* in pain, then resistance to that fact will only make the suffering worse.

Pain is obviously meant to be a warning sign and it aims to keep us safe. It is a call to action. The problem is that if we become over-reactive to it, we become fearful of it. This becomes very limiting for us. We can end up avoiding life, fearful of doing anything that might bring pain. Learning not to fear pain will give you much more freedom to enjoy life. It will significantly reduce much of your avoidable suffering.

The practice of meditation can totally transform your relationship with experiencing pain, which, let's be honest, we are all likely to experience as part of being human. It has given me the confidence to not need to avoid pain. It has also enabled me to stay more detached to it as I go through it. Even the most intense pain becomes more bearable and possible to completely dissolve when in states of higher consciousness. Let me use the difficult emotions that I experienced after splitting up with my husband as an example.

When I would sit to meditate when in the grip of these emotions, this is what typically happened for me…

As I would first sit and try to connect to my breath, I would be in a very uncomfortable state. I would feel bereft, empty and heartbroken, and was usually in tears. I would try to focus on my breath but my emotions would continue to overwhelm me. I would feel like I wanted to end the meditation and go and distract myself but I would stay with my practice, however uncomfortable.

I might have some frustration surface; past memories; he said/she said stuff; thoughts of him being with someone else; of me not being with him. All of these uncomfortable thoughts and feelings would be circulating. As would any physical discomfort that went with them – pain in my chest, tightness in my jaw, the gripping of my stomach or tension across my face. All had become frequent visitors at that time. I would keep bringing myself back to the breath, which took considerable effort.

Sooner or later though, I would eventually feel the feelings start to loosen their grip a little. Often I would find myself grabbing hold of them all again – not quite ready to let them go. I would return to my breath. Usually, if I continued, a subtle level of peace would start to creep in. My thoughts, emotions and any physical discomfort would all start to settle down. The peace would begin to increase and with it a feeling of love that wrapped itself around any remaining discomfort.

At no point would I attempt to push thoughts or feelings away. I would allow it all to show up. I would cry if that's what was there, without attempting to stop. Eventually, all discomfort would cease – not by trying to make it, but by surrendering to it. Relief, followed by peace and love, would be eventually all that I felt. It would be the calm after the storm. Though my human egoic self was still present, my higher self would seemingly completely have engulfed it. Love had dissolved my fear and pain, for the time being at least.

Unlike distraction, which often is the mere parking and suppressing of emotions, during meditation I have found that feelings and emotions pass through me until they dissolve. Meditation, for me at least, has helped bring about genuine healing, rather than a temporary diversion.

I have also used meditation to surrender to physical pain too. It allows me to be in non-resistance to it, which in turn reduces the level of suffering. Mindfulness meditation is now mainstream for its potential benefits in coping with pain and long-term illness. Much of this was developed by pioneering mindfulness leader, Jon Kabat-Zinn, whose Mindfulness Based Stress Reduction programme has helped thousands of patients to cope with chronic pain and illness. Considerable research around this area has been done at his Stress Reduction Clinic at the University of Massachusetts Medical Centre. I highly recommend checking out his work.

Interestingly, this ability to sit with my own pain has also given me the ability to sit with others in their pain. I used to find that very difficult. I would feel their pain so deeply myself that I often found it overwhelming, which meant I wasn't much use to them. Now I have a far greater ability to stay centred, which allows me to offer comfort and steadiness to others in the midst of their own storms.

Whether it be physical, mental or emotional pain, the practice of breath awareness, meditation and a connection to higher consciousness can enable us to stay connected to a deep level of peace even amid pain.

If you want to experiment with this yourself, next time you find yourself to be in unavoidable discomfort:

- Bring your attention to the breath. Breathe. Make your exhalation a second or two longer than your inhalation.
- Try to accept that the pain is there, and that you don't have to waste any of your energy fighting it being there. Let whatever is showing up be there.
- Comfort yourself. What do you need to support you in this pain? Can your own-best-friend-self wrap you in love?
- Breathe. Let go. Breathe. Let go. Breathe.
- Know that it will pass.

## Non-grasping of joy

It is odd to think that even joy can be a cause of stress, but it can be for many reasons. We can spoil our enjoyment of many things by worrying about them ending. I have worked with people that are frightened when things are going well for them. Their enjoyment is tainted by them living in fear that something will go wrong at some point.

Even when fear isn't involved, we can curtail our enjoyment of something because we know it won't last. Have you ever wasted the last few days of a holiday because you know you are going home soon? Imagine the craziness of not enjoying a holiday while we are still on it! A week's holiday can feel like a four-day holiday if we fall into that trap. It's where being present in the moment comes in again. We are where we mentally choose to be. If we can allow ourselves to be fully present in the moment then we are free to experience joy more fully. We can embrace it while it is there, rather than focusing on it soon ending.

Another way that joy can cause stress is in how we chase after things that bring us pleasure. The chasing after of what we think will bring us pleasure is usually a fruitless game because not long after we have what we chased after, we become bored and chase after the next thing. And so the endless cycle of needing to have that which brings us pleasure continues. It doesn't matter if it's the latest fashion, phone, handbag, car, affair or holiday. Needing to have the latest this, that or the other, for example, can bring a level of discomfort until we get it. It can also get us into financial debt because we can't control our urges or desires.

Sometimes we value things that give us pleasure disproportionately. We can become too attached to them. Take getting a new car, for example. That can be stressful for some. If you are so pleased with your shiny new car that you become paranoid about it getting marked in any way, then even a trip to the local supermarket can create stress with the fear that someone might open a car door into it.

The irony is that the less attached to things we are, the more we can enjoy them. The moment we become attached, we bring in what yoga philosophy calls grasping; we cling to it for fear of losing it. Or, as Yoda wisely said: 'Train yourself to let go of everything you fear to lose'. Romantic

189

relationships can be a good example of this. If we fear being hurt, we won't allow ourselves to go all in and experience the joy of love, just in case the relationship fails.

Through a connection to your higher self, you will recognize that all of life is transient, and that the only constant is the ever-loving, ever-peaceful, ever-joyful being that you are. When you recognize yourself as that, you don't need to find it in anything or anyone else, and thereafter ends your grasping. It doesn't mean that you won't experience pleasure and joy through others or other things, but you won't *need* them to bring it.

What do you grasp too tightly in life? What would it feel like to loosen your grip on them? Can you appreciate them being there without having a fear of losing them?

Ultimately, everything in life will all come and go. Pain will come and go. Pleasure will come and go. Learning to ride the waves of both the pleasures and pains of life through non-attachment will bring you immense freedom. It will enable you to enjoy life's pleasures without a need to grasp them tightly. You will not fear pain because it will be wrapped with comfort and love.

I, personally, have come to realize that the experience of being human is wasted if it is numbed out and avoided. If we want a fulfilling life, we must be open to all of it. When we open ourselves to it all, having connected to our higher self, we will realize that we have nothing to fear. We neither need to run from pain nor grab hold of pleasure. All will find us in its own good time, and when it does, we will be more than equipped to meet it.

# # The hack

Know that all of life is transient. Pain and pleasure will come and go. Enjoy the pleasures and joy when they come your way. Be grateful for them, fully present in them and embrace every moment they are there. Know that you are brave enough to sit with whatever pain comes your way. Don't resist it or avoid it. You are equipped to meet everything that you face in life, and have nothing to fear.

# WE'RE IN THIS TOGETHER

Have you ever noticed what happens in a traffic jam when an ambulance needs to get through? How every single driver, within a matter of seconds, and without so much as a single word, manages to synchronize movement in unity with every other driver on the road to create the space for the ambulance to get by?

Have you ever been moved to tears watching a TV documentary covering the lives of a family ripped apart by terminal illness?

Equally, have you been moved to tears and admiration by seeing someone triumph over extreme hardship to get to a better place?

Or been humbled by the lengths that one human being will go to, to reduce the suffering of another?

And have you noticed just how much money can be raised overnight when an appeal is made in a crisis?

All of this happens because it is a fundamental part of our human nature to care for each other. It isn't that we *want* to care for each other – we *do* care for each other. It is a fundamental part of our human nature to want to help, where help is needed. As is wanting to pull together, not apart. We don't need to try to be collaborative; we *are* collaborative. It isn't that we need to learn to be generous;

WE'RE IN THIS TOGETHER

we *are* generous. We don't need to try to *be* kind, because
we *are* kind. And the only reason we want to love and be
loved is because we *are* love.

Kindness is everything. I don't say that lightly.

How does kindness show up in everyday life? Perhaps
it's generosity. Thoughtfulness. Friendliness. Consideration.
Patience. Forgiveness. Tolerance. Gentleness. Encouragement.

I am sure there are many more ways that it shows up,
all of which make the world a better place. When kindness
is present, all of life is better. I genuinely believe that it is
our true nature, at every level, to be kind. We only abandon
our ability to be kind when we are suffering in some way.
How can we *choose* to be unkind, unless we are somehow
suffering?

Even the most challenging and unbearable of situations
can be made better through kindness. We need look no
further than Viktor Frankl's book, *Man's Search for Meaning*,
to find evidence of this. In it, he describes his experience
as a prisoner in Nazi concentration camps during World
War II. He demonstrates that even under the most horrific
circumstances, we still choose our response to life. He said:

> Everything can be taken from a man but one thing:
> the last of the human freedoms—to choose one's
> attitude in any given set of circumstances, to choose
> one's own way.[16]

You will infinitely reduce your stress, and the stress of
others, if you practise kindness.

---

[16] V. Frankl, *Man's search for meaning*, 2004, p. 86.

Your job, above all else, is to remember who you are. It is to remember that, despite the stress that you feel, you are more than that. You are not your impatience, your anger or your anxiety. You never could be. Don't ever forget that. No matter what we face, choosing to be kind to ourselves and to others is a gift that will always make the world a better place.

## # The hack

We are all here to work *with* each other, not *against* one another. We are here to help each other, not just ourselves. We are here because we choose to contribute to the world that we live in, together, as best we can.

Kindness is key. In every moment. With yourself. With others. With everything. Enough said.

# THE WORLD IS YOUR MIRROR

Feedback comes to us in many magical ways. Life itself has a way of reflecting back to us the lens with which we are viewing it. If we pay attention it will reveal our blind spots. It will show us our internal state, our beliefs and our mindset.

Here are some examples as food for thought…

- If you are someone that shows kindness to others, you will likely find that the world is full of others reflecting kindness back to you.
- If you are generous, you will likely find that you live in abundance.
- If you choose to be your own-worst-enemy-self, you will likely find that the world is full of enemies.
- If you are impatient, you will likely find a world full of things to be impatient about.
- If you are fearful, you will likely find plenty to fear.
- If you are stressed, you will likely find plenty to get stressed about.
- If you are grateful, you will likely have much to appreciate.
- If you are supportive, you will likely find that you are surrounded by support.

- If you feel like a victim, you will likely have plenty of opportunities to be one.
- If you feel lacking, you will likely never have enough.
- If you seek out opportunities to help others, you will likely always find the help that you need.
- If you choose to be your own-best-friend-self, you will never feel alone again.
- If you choose to be love, you will likely find that your world is filled with it.

As novelist Anaïs Nin said: 'We don't see things as they are, we see them as we are'.[17]

What is it that you see in your world? Don't judge yourself for what you find; just notice it, and know that it's within your power to change whatever you want to – as #hack 50 will cover.

> # **# The hack**
>
> Reflect on what your world is trying to show you. What is it reflecting back to you about your mindset, your beliefs and your internal state of being? What blind spots can it reveal to you?

---

[17] A. Nin, *Seduction of the Minotaur*, 1961, p. 124.

# SHIFTING YOUR INTERNAL STATE

I know that I am a far better person when I meditate regularly. It enables me to be the loving, kind and generous person that I want to be. When I am that person, I know I bring my best to the world and to those around me. When my internal state is a loving, kind and generous one, I notice that life flows that bit more. Synchronicity, abundance and joy become everyday life. Without doubt, my outer world reflects my inner one.

Life has taught me that the single most important thing I can do is to look after my own internal state of being. Everything depends on it. Without meaning to sound overly dramatic, the world depends on it. So many people feel a pressure to find their purpose in life, and I can tell you that the biggest purpose, and achievement, that any of us can bring to our world is to master our own internal state.

Stress can ignite the human egoic self into selfishness and a lack mentality. We do not bring the best of ourselves to the world when we come from that limited place. We know that. If you take one thing away from reading this book, then please know that there is nothing at all selfish about looking after yourself so that you can be the loving, kind and giving person that you are. Find whatever method you need to overcome your limiting mindsets, beliefs and fears.

As #hack 49 suggested, you really are creating your world, our world. There is a balance to be found between all that we do outwardly, and all that we are inwardly. The inner journey is one that joins up all the dots. If you want to find love in your outer world, you must connect to it inwardly. If you want peace in your outer world, you must go inside to find it. If you want to change your outer world, you must do so from within.

## How to change

I have written this entire book to offer simple strategies to help you to change your internal state. The way to change your world is to start living the change you seek. You have to commit to taking the next step, which is sometimes incredibly small. In all the work that I have done over the years, both on myself and with others, I have found that it is the small, seemingly insignificant, steps that prove to be the most effective and lasting. That's why I am a complete advocate of anything being better than nothing. All of it is worth it.

Small steps are also realistic. If you are currently stressed out, it won't help at all for me to say *just start being happy and everything will be fine*. If you could do that, you wouldn't be stressed and you wouldn't be reading this book. So, don't try to make a giant leap from feeling shit to feeling amazing. It might just happen that way for some of you but, if it doesn't, that's totally OK. And it's perfectly possible to change your internal state, one step at a time.

It's about momentum. So start small. Start with what you can do. And then keep going, as best you can.

Recall my top three tips from #hack 44 for mastering the internal state:

1. Breathe
2. Get present
3. Be your own-best-friend-self

From there, it's a case of *actually applying* any of the relevant #hacks from this book, or from any other advice you find helpful, to your life. It's about doing the work. As best you can. Remember, anything is always better than nothing.

If you're trying to lose weight and exercise more, walking around the block for ten minutes is better than staying on the sofa thinking about doing an hour in the gym. If you want to feel less anxious, taking ten conscious deep breaths is better than meaning to do an hour of meditation. If you want to find love, joining an online dating site and going on a few disappointing dates is better than hoping your dream partner will turn up.

You see, by showing up in the world as a willing participant in our own life, there really is magic in it, as is so beautifully put by the mountaineer and writer W. H. Murray:

Whatever you can do or dream you can, begin it; boldness has genius, power, and magic in it.[18]

---

[18] W. H. Murray, *The Scottish Himalayan expedition*, 1951. This quotation is widely attributed to Johann Wolfgang von Goethe (including by Murray himself) but is in fact taken from a very loose translation of Goethe's *Faust* by John Anster in 1835.

Do the internal work, take inspired action from that place and watch just how easily your external world begins to change.

## # The hack

Make your internal state your number-one priority. Above all else. Master it by doing the internal work. Breathe, get present, be your own-best-friend-self and take action from that inspired place. Anything is always better than nothing. No matter how small the step.

# AFTERWORD

In both the life you are living right now, and in all of your future plans, goals and dreams, there is one thing that will serve you very well in keeping stress at bay. And that is to keep things very simple. Take one day at a time. In all of your busyness, working towards all that you will work towards, take it all one day at a time. If that's too much, do it one hour at a time. And if you're still overwhelmed, do it one minute at a time. Most importantly of all, do it one moment at a time. In the very moment you are in.

You'll get there. You will always get there.

It is my greatest hope that this book has served to remind you of your true nature. It is my hope that it has helped to reduce your suffering, so that you in turn can reduce someone else's. If I can help you in any other way, then please do visit my website www.louiselloyd.life

We are all in this together. If we can all learn to be more present in each moment, we will have a chance of remembering who we truly are. If we can be more present in each moment, we will choose not to add to another's suffering. In fact, we will go out of our way to reduce it. We won't be too busy. We won't forget why we are here, or that we are here for each other.

It really doesn't matter what we are doing or where we are. What matters is who we are choosing to be. What matters is that we remember we are love, and that it is our gift to share that with everyone we meet.

This brings me to the most important #hack of the book. In any given moment, there is only one question we ever need ask ourselves, to guide our every move. That question is:

# *What would love do now?*